W9-CDD-068

THE REDEMPTION
A Personalist View

THE REDEMPTION
A Personalist View

by
Marcel van Caster, S.J.

Translated by
Eileen O'Gorman, R.S.C.J.
and
Olga Guedatarian

DEUS BOOKS
PAULIST PRESS
(PAULIST FATHERS)
Glen Rock, N.J.

A Deus Books Edition of Paulist Press, 1965, by special arrangement with La Pensée Catholique, Brussels, Belgium.

The original edition: *La Redemption sitúee dans une perspective personnaliste* was adapted by the author and translated by Eileen O'Gorman, R.S.C.J. (Chaps. I-IV) and Olga Guedatarian (Chap. V).

De Superiorum Ordinis Licentia
NIHIL OBSTAT: Robert E. Hunt, S.T.D.
Censor Librorum

IMPRIMATUR: ✠ Thomas A. Boland, S.T.D.
Archbishop of Newark

July 12, 1965

The Nihil Obstat and Imprimatur are official declarations that a book or pamphlet is free of doctrinal or moral error. No implication is contained therein that those who granted the Nihil Obstat and Imprimatur agree with the contents, opinions or statements expressed.

Copyright © 1965 by
The Missionary Society
of St. Paul the Apostle
in the State of New York

Library of Congress
Catalog Card Number: 65-26793

COVER DESIGN: Claude Ponsot

Published by Paulist Press
Editorial Office: 304 West 58th St., N.Y., N.Y. 10019
Business Office: Glen Rock, New Jersey, 07452

Printed and Bound in the United States of America

CONTENTS

CHAPTER II

ANALYSIS AND COMMENTARY

CHAPTER III

SYNTHESIS AND CATECHETICAL CONCLUSIONS

CHAPTER IV

FURTHER EXAMINATION OF CERTAIN ELEMENTS OF THE SYNTHESIS

CHAPTER V

A CONTEMPORARY EXPLANATION OF HUMAN CONDITIONING FACTORS

FOREWORD

Every Christian, and in a very particular way every catechist, is called upon to penetrate the meaning of his faith, to bear witness to it before men, and to refute defective interpretations of its truths when they are presented.

It is for these reasons that we envisage a two-fold *usefulness* for the following pages: they will be profitable for personal reflection and for catechesis. On the one hand, they make a positive response to the *difficulties, whether explicit or implicit,* which concern the essence of the Redemption, difficulties which stem from inaccurate interpretations, difficulties which are sometimes presented as belonging to the very content of faith, and thus give rise to grave problems for the catechist. On the other hand, they present a concrete application of the catechetical principle according to which instruction penetrates below the surface of the words, shuns all deviations, and is based on *personalist realities.* As for the formulas in which these realities are expressed, "they are texts to be interpreted in their context"; *texts* that are biblical in origin, a *context* that is as much existential and cultural as it is bound up with worship and literary forms.

This principle of interpretation also determines the method we will follow. Revelation is progressive. Each text and its particular context finds its total significance against the background of salvation history. It is important, therefore, to consider the theme of redemption through the progress of ideas and expressions that develop in relationship with the progressive realization of salvation. We do this by presenting Redemption from the point of view of its origin in history and in thought (Chapter I).

The expressions used in the course of this development require a particular interpretation that will clarify the meaning of the different analogies and make explicit the way in which they should be understood. This is the analytical commentary (Chapter II).

A synthesis accompanies the conclusions which can be drawn for Catechesis (Chapter III).

The very importance of the subject calls for complete understanding of, and the greatest possible light on, the important phases of the question. Chapter IV is concerned with a more extensive examination of certain points of the synthesis.

Finally, we examine the terms in which the encounter between the mystery of salvation and the contemporary mind is presented. What does redemption in Jesus Christ mean for modern man? (Chapter V).

MARCEL VAN CASTER, S.J.

CHAPTER I

GENETIC PRESENTATION

The Economy of Redemption in Salvation History

The whole of the divine economy, by which we mean the relations that God establishes between man and himself, assumes the form of a collaboration in which every initiative belongs to God, and man is called upon to make a constant and positive response. When mediators have a role to play in this process, it will consist in "representing" the divine action and in "provoking and representing" man's response. It is possible to discern the principal stages of this economy.

I. PREPARATION

1. *Yahweh and His People*

The Old Testament is directly concerned with the relations between Yahweh and his people. The introductory chapters are intended to throw light on the situations which follow, but it is also true to say that their meaning becomes clear only in the light of the experience of the Hebrew people. Now this experience is

13

centered upon the event of the first "redemption" of the people of Israel: the deliverance out of Egypt, the sojourn in the desert—where God concludes his alliance with his people—and the entrance into the promised land.

In this event the predominant part taken by God determines the part he expects from the people.

It is Yahweh who redeems Israel. When they use this term, the sacred writers are expressing the twofold aspect of a single reality: the aspect of power and the aspect of difficulty. Yahweh is the *Go'el,* the one who gives protection to his own in time of distress; he "saves", and, in so doing, he is accomplishing a difficult work: he pays a "ransom."

We must note immediately that the reality is expressed by a symbol which we cannot treat as we would treat a "notional definition". In other words, the symbol is valid only for certain imaginative elements which have meaning in the context, but we cannot draw conclusions from it apart from these elements. For example, we cannot ask "to whom" the ransom is paid; it is not paid to anyone. The word signifies rather the onerous conditions of the deliverance and that it is a work accomplished with power. "He bears our burdens, the God who is our salvation" (Ps. 67, 20). And Yahweh does this because he is faithful and for the glory of his name.

As for *the people's part,* it consists in accepting Yahweh's deliverance. The carrying out of the rite ordained by God was the sign of this acceptance. And they were to bear with courage and confidence the difficulties inherent in the march to freedom.

As they left Egypt the Hebrews felt only physical and social distress; soon they were to have the experience of moral distress. The blood of the paschal lamb was not related to sin, but the blood of the sacrifices of purification would be. How was this *deliverance from sin* to be effected?

Sin consists in the *infidelity* of the people. But Yahweh remains faithful, even when the people as a nation are unfaithful to him. In delivering from sin, it is once again God who takes the initiative of this form of "redemption": "It is the Lord who shall redeem Israel from all their iniquities" (Ps. 129). Sin has roused the "anger" of Yahweh. This term expresses the opposition which, in God, confronts a refusal on the part of man, and the divine will to correct the situation.

To this end God sends his "punishments", but these are primarily intended to bring about the *conversion* of the sinner, not his destruction. It is only when men obstinately refuse to be converted that the anger of Yahweh shows itself as a force for perdition. Therefore, men should see in the punishment of their sins God's call to conversion, and, under the influence of God's faithful love, they should return to him so as to receive his forgiveness.

For *God* is always ready to be merciful to the man who is not hardened in sin. He manifests his "propitiation" in the blood-rite (*asham*). Here we are considering a means that God furnishes to his people. In fact, blood belongs to God; it is sacred to him; this is why, with God's permission, it can serve as a means of purification or *reconciliation,* of resanctification, of expiation, (all these terms are synonymous).

The *people* on their side, once turned away from their sin, implore the divine pardon and thank Yahweh for having given (allowed the use of) blood in the form of ritual aspersion, as a means of purification (Lev. 17, 11).

At first there was no very clear distinction between the purely legal plane of involuntary transgression and the moral plane; nor was there a distinction between the guilt of sin and the guilt of punishment, between the collective and the individual. On the other hand, the idea of sacrifice is easily distorted. This is the case when men imagine that, in a ritual ceremony, they are furnishing God with gifts he needs, and that they can thus, independently of their moral dispositions, obtain favors from him, such as the withdrawal of his punishments.

Real progress takes place with *interiorization,* which puts the emphasis on the dispositions of the heart (Ps. 49), and with *personalization,* which takes cognizance of the fact that a man is not formally punished for the sin of another man (Ez. 18, 4.23). These two elements of progress should in no way suppress the value of the rite, or of the sense of participation by the community. This last is all the more important in that the economy of the mystery of salvation comprises the role of mediators whom God appoints.

2. *Mediators in the Redemption of Israel, and in particular the "Servant of Yahweh"*

God acts through men who are the bearers of his word and his power. In general, and in a certain sense, they also represent the people before God.

At the period of the Exodus, *Moses* united rather indistinctly in his own person the various forms of mediation: he speaks in the name of Yahweh; he is the political and military leader of his people; he carries out the sacrificial rite of the covenant; he intercedes for the sinful nation.

In the subsequent centuries there is a differentiation of these roles. The kings, as the "anointed" of the Lord,

are the *liberators* of their people because they ensure
for them victory over their enemies; or, they are unfaithful to him whom they represent and whom they must obey
in their exercise of power. The *priests* are the *inter-
cessors*; they atone for sin when they carry out the rites
of purification. But it is the *prophets* who soon come to
play the principal role of mediator. For they are the
heralds of God, proclaiming his will, his indignation,
and his mercy, and they are also "the waking points" of
the conscience of the people.

The existential situation of the prophets is a paradox.
For it is in their own moral and religious judgment that
the infidelity of the people of whom they are a part
takes on its meaning in the light that God communicates
to them; and it is because of the testimony they render
to God and to the conscience of their brethren that they
are rejected and persecuted by their fellow-countrymen.
They are, therefore, called upon to assume a redemptive
role, and we find in them the two aspects of this role:
(1) as bearers of God's Word, they are endowed with
the power proper to this Word and they bring freedom
from "ignorance of God"; (2) but, to remain faithful to
this role, they must face opposition and persecution; in
this way they pay the price for their work: it is accomplished under difficult conditions.

At the end of the period of the exile, the confidence
and hope of Israel are to be found expressed intensively
in the songs of the "Servant of Yahweh". The interpretation of these songs poses a serious problem even today.
Do they concern a single person? or several? of the people as a whole? a king, a priest, or a prophet? At what
period did he live? What did he do? What happened to
him?

Whatever the case, he sums up in his own person the

different forms of redemption we have mentioned: he is
invested with God's power and his meekness; he proclaims God's will, and, it may be, imposes it as lawgiver.
He is confronted by the sin of his people in those who
persecute him, and, in bearing the weight of sin in its
painful effects. Seizing its detestable character in all
the anguish of this experience, he pays the ransom necessary for his work. Persevering to the end, he offers his
life as *asham*: when his blood is shed it is assimilated to
the ritual shedding of blood in the sacrifice of purification. Then he is saved by God. It may be that he also
contemplates God's face in the sacred light of the
temple. He receives (that he may govern them) the
nations who have been reestablished in justice.

What is his principal characteristic in all this? It is
fidelity to his mission, especially to the mission he has
received to awaken the consciences of men to a new
appeal from God. Now his fidelity triumphs in that
supreme trial which is the result of the infidelity of his
people; this makes it possible for the Servant to give the
ultimate proof of his fidelity; therefore, it "represents"
the conversion to which he calls his people in the Lord's
name.

And so it is the fidelity of the Servant that receives its
reward in the reestablishment of the fidelity of the multitudes of men to the one Lord of all. He is the Servant
"strong and meek", because faithful; the "suffering"
Servant, because he is faithful; the "glorified" Servant,
because he is faithful (*see* page 116).

This picture of the Servant-Redeemer receives its
complement in the picture of the "Son of Man" coming
on the clouds (*i.e.,* invested with divine power), to
"save" (wholly and definitively) men who truly await
their salvation from Yahweh, the "poor", (those perse-

cuted for justice' sake), for he comes to render the "judgment" of God.

II. REALIZATION

At the prophetic junction of the Old and the New Testaments appears *John the Baptist*. Very concretely he summons men to conversion because the real Messiah is at hand. He points him out. But his own concept of the role of Jesus is to undergo an evolution, because it is Jesus himself who will fully reveal what his function is, as he accomplishes his work.

1. *The Official Inauguration of His Mission Makes the Situation Clear.*

As previously in the work of redemption, God acts and calls upon man to collaborate with him. The Mediator par excellence, "he who is to come", will act in the name of God and in the name of men.

In the ceremony of *the Baptism of Jesus on the banks of the Jordan,* it is clear that it is the Father who sends him and that Jesus accepts his mission. This mission involves a part to be played *in an existential situation,* whose meaning is emphasized by the context. What is the significance of the water of the Jordan, especially at this spot? What is the significance for Jesus of participation in a baptism designed for sinners?

The answer to the first question is very clear: by going down into the Jordan at the spot where the Hebrews, led by Joshua, crossed the river to enter the promised land, *Jesus takes his place, according to the mission which he has received from the Father, at the head of the new people of God, so that by following him they may enter the promised land of perfect union with God.* This *situation of men who have been called* includes the requirement of fidelity under temptation. So Jesus goes *into the desert,* there to undergo the trials that marked the journey of the Hebrews and in which they succumbed to infidelity, but in which he, the Christ, will remain faithful to his mission.

The second question is much more difficult to answer. What is the meaning of the action of Jesus, allowing himself to be baptized under the conditions in which John the Baptist was administering a baptism of penance? The somewhat ambiguous words of John the Baptist will only be clearly understood later on. We have here the *talia* —a word that can mean either *servant* or *lamb*—who *bears* (supports the weight, but which weight?) and/or *takes away*—it is again the same word—the sin of the world. As for the reality with which the gesture and the words are dealing, the fact is that Jesus is in no sense a sinner, and he is not considered to be one by the heavenly Father who wills this baptism.

Jesus needs neither repentance nor conversion, for he has no part in the guilt of sinners. But he comes *to enter by participation into the situation of men who are sinners,* in a way that will only become apparent as a result of the very deeds he will do and the words he will pronounce in order to accomplish his mission.

2. *Establishment of Definitive Positions*

What Jesus first of all establishes in his public life is the fact that he is acting in God's name. We find united in his person the three forms of mediator-redeemer invested with divine power that appeared in the Old Testament. But Jesus realizes them in so transcendant a manner as to astound his contemporaries. In fact, the preaching of Jesus is not only carried out "with authority", it is accompanied by bodily cures and the remission of sins. As a redeemer invested with divine power, Jesus exercises it with a generosity to all. This manifests God's goodness to man. The devotedness of Jesus is a sign of the solicitude of God in the person of his envoy. And the price, which has to be paid by those who act as God's envoys, Jesus will soon feel to be a very heavy one by reason of the opposition of men.

Before going into details, we should note briefly that in his public life Jesus is also acting in our name.

Participating in our human situation, Jesus realizes to perfection the vocation God gives to men, which consists in responding to his love. He does so when he meets his Father in prayer, there to praise him and offer him petitions in our name; he does so in showing men a personal and effective love. If, therefore, the activity, which God expects of man in the work of the salvation of the human race, consists in receiving the gift he wishes to make to man, and in putting into practice the gift received so as to live in charity, Jesus never wavered in giving this response in our name. And his fidelity acted as a corrective to that movement of infidelity that was developing in mankind. And this mission of Christ's response, reestablishing humanity in its response to God, is going to achieve its fullness when the decisive "hour" comes.

What that hour will be we can see little by little as the public life of Jesus runs its course, notably in its relation to the reactions that confront him in his contemporaries, "types", moreover, of the categories of men who reappear in one generation after the other and in every country under the sun.

This new life to which Jesus summons them, poses, for those who see and hear him, the *exigencies of a conversion* they are not prepared to meet. And when Jesus, in the last phases of the divine revelation he brings

to men, makes known to them the unique—and transcendant—nature of his role and his person, *instead of
faith* he is met with *the rejection of his message and
his person.*

It is precisely the confrontation with the opposition
of men, it is their "infidelity" in the face of God's most
sublime appeal, which is to constitute "the most critical
and intense aspect of the situation". And it is in this
critical situation that Christ the redeemer will give the
supreme testimony of fidelity, the fidelity of the loving
mercy of his Father to all men, and of the fidelity looked
for by the Father from men. This double fidelity Christ
will show in his "hour".

3. *The "Hour" of Jesus-Redeemer*

The act forming the center of the work of redemption
is so rich in meaning that we will have to consider it
from several different angles, complementary to each
other, in order to understand its essence. According to
the method we are using, we will consider: (a) the
synthesis of the "hour" celebrated in the eucharist; (b)
the aspect of death, realized on the cross; (c) the
aspect of life, manifested in the resurrection; (d) a
summation in terms of generosity and love: Jesus gives
his life.

(a) *The Redemption Celebrated in the Eucharist*

In the economy of salvation it is usual for the celebration of an event *to follow* its realization in the historical order. However, every celebration also has a
certain turning toward the future. When Jesus took his
place at the table with his disciples, with the intention
of transforming the Jewish passover into the Christian
eucharist, he did so "knowing that his hour had come"
(Jn. 13). This hour is the hour of "passing out of this

world to his Father"; hence, it is indissolubly the hour of his death and resurrection.

Since it was to bring the realization of the redemption, this hour is above all others the one in which God himself is at work. Therefore, *the glory of God* is manifested; in it all men will be able to share, and this will be their *perfect joy*.

Jesus places the eucharistic meal in this clear eschatological perspective. This same reality is found expressed in the terms of the "New Testament" which is concluded in the sacrifice of *communion,* of which Jesus here institutes the "memorial". And his blood of the covenant (the sacrifice of communion) will be at the same time the blood of the sacrifice of *purification,* for it is shed for the remission of sins. The disciples who participate in this celebration, will later understand better what existential participation it makes possible and requires.

(b) *Death on the Cross*

For men without faith the cross of Christ is above all a folly and a scandal: a folly, because it means not willing to evade persecution; a scandal, because it indicates that the wicked have deprived the good of their means of action.

In reality, and for men enlightened by the Holy Spirit—though even here they must exert themselves to go beyond the limits of their "natural" judgment—those who put Christ to death and who committed the evil are not the principal actors in the events that took place on Calvary. For in accepting death, Jesus is more active than they are, and Jesus himself is acting in total dependence on the Father, who, through his Son, is acting for our good, and who, from his Son, accepts the loving response of humanity. "In Christ he reconciled the world to himself" (2 Cor. 5, 19).

On the cross, as elsewhere, it is first of all *on behalf of the Father* that Jesus acts. The Father and the Son are one, even in their confrontation with the onerous situation caused by sinners, and into which the Son has entered as the Father's envoy. In the patience of the Son the Father wills to show the strength of his patient love. But the defeat the Son suffers on the immediate and terrestrial plane, is in fact, on the super-terrestrial and future plane, a victory of the power of God. For God has made of Christ who has shed his blood, a "means of purification" for our sins, that is, a source of reconsecration for converted sinners. "Christ crucified, the power of God and the wisdom of God" (1 Cor. 1, 24. 30). Christ on the Cross is the *instrument of divine power,* manifesting in the application the efficacy of God's merciful love for us.

Again, in accepting death Jesus acts also *on behalf of men* with respect to God. He responds to the Father's expectations, and this response he gives in the name of all of us. It consists in remaining faithful to the functioning of charity among men. Jesus is "obedient even unto the death on the cross", that is, he remains faithful to charity even in the supreme trial, even in the final and most difficult situation.

This fidelity on the part of Jesus effects *the reestablishment of humanity in its response to God*. It is realized in *the Head* of the human race, and at the same time it is *an appeal to all the members,* in view of their personal participation. This reestablishment has three dimensions: it restores the link between man and God (the intersubjective dimension); it redeems man from the slavery of sin and gives him access to salvation (subjective dimension); and it repairs the damage to the glory of God effected by sin (the objective dimension).

The fidelity of Jesus on the cross does all of this in a perfect manner. For it is:

—fidelity *carried to its highest pitch*. Jesus is faithful to the end; he shows the intensity of his love by manifesting it under the greatest difficulties;

—fidelity which *compensates* and makes reparation in its confrontation with sin for two reasons, one of which is concerned with the role of temptation, the other, with the effect of the scandal. First, *the attitude of Jesus in trial and temptation* is most radically opposed to that of the sinner. Where man yields to temptation because he reacts to the test with proud self-sufficiency, or with discouragement in the face of the difficulty of remaining faithful, Jesus for his part remains faithful in temptation with humble confidence in his Father. Secondly, *the public evidence* of charity which Jesus gives on the cross effectively opposes the scandal given by sin. The disorder brought into the world by the scandal of sin finds its rebuttal in the faithful witness which, from the cross of Jesus, streams out over the world. The victory won by the cross over the scandal stemming from the influence of sin, will only be total because the witness of Jesus is not lost in defeat, but opens up new perspectives. It is important to insist that these are part and parcel of this final characteristic of fidelity in charity.

—a *fidelity directed toward total communion*. Jesus accepts his death as the first movement of his "return to the Father"; the second will be the final welcome and the continual reciprocal gift in eternal life. The fidelity of Jesus on the cross is the fidelity of charity, which is conscious of the fact that it is dynamically oriented toward perfect *communion of life*. The sacrifice of the

cross is not merely a sacrifice of purification, of reparation for sin, it is at the same time *the first movement
of the sacrifice of communion* in which Jesus lives
eternally and to which he wishes to integrate us more
and more perfectly until the consummation of the redemption.

Jesus on the cross is not merely, from God's point of
view, the instrument of our redemption from sin; he is
also, for men, *the locus of the fidelity of reparation,
the starting point, for the whole human race, of the
return to the Father,* with a view to perfect communion
of life (see pp. 21–22).

(c) *New Life in the Resurrection*

Redemption ensures *salvation*. If the first of these
terms conveys the idea of "deliverance from evil" and
the second has above all the idea of "a good restored",
the two terms, in our present situation, have a negative
and a positive aspect. Therefore, we have an inadequate
idea of the redemption if we consider only the first
of these aspects. It is essential to see redemption in the
totality of its positive meaning.

In terms of events, this means that the "Hour" of
Jesus is the hour of his death-and-resurrection. The
orientation of the cross to the resurrection is essential
to the death of Jesus; it is as much a constitutive element
of it as the experience of the suffering. The resurrection
is not a supplement, added to the redemptive cross;
rather, it is its complement, and without it the redemption would lose its most important meaning.

Once again, it is God who is the principal agent. He
raises up Jesus from the dead. The work of the risen
Jesus is henceforth to manifest the glory of the Father
in the new situation proper to the person of the incarnate Son. Thus, he fulfills in a more emphatic way

his role of envoy, acting *on God's behalf* with respect to men, and in so doing the risen Christ splendidly reveals *the creative force of the new life* which the Father is inaugurating. He manifests God's triumph over his enemies and the fact that he has already realized in his Son the accomplishment of his plan for the salvation of all men. God's goodness is stronger than death, whose power comes from sin; the mercy of God restores life under new and better conditions.

More than ever before, Christ acts, too, *on behalf of men* before God. His is an *active receptivity in the name of all mankind.* He receives the everlasting fullness of salvation, and he is made capable of effectively communicating the strength of his charity and the seed of immortality to all men, his brethren.

Therefore, in his glorious life Christ completes what he began on the cross. There, the redemption was already rendered positive in the reestablishment of the faithful response of the human race.

Now this response is in no sense the end of a dialogue; on the contrary, it is the condition of *the continuing dialogue* between God and man. In this response, the Father reestablishes and raises to greater perfection the "dialogue-of-life": the Son is "graced" with risen life, which, through him, is given by participation to all men. The whole of redemption, realized by Christ, is *an effective appeal to our participation.* We are called to respond with him and to live fully with him.

Before examining the various modes of the redemption continued in the Church, it will be useful to sum up what we have already said in terms of generous love.

(d) *The Father Gives His Son; the Son Gives His Life*

Before the incarnation, from all eternity the Father communicates his own life to his Son, and the Son responds to this gift with love in the unity of the Spirit. When the Son becomes man, the charity that flows through his humanity is also a gift of the Father. The entire redemption is based on this gift. But here the word *to give* has several different meanings, each of which has a negative and a positive aspect.

First of all, we may speak of the gift God gives to men.

The Father gives us his Son: negatively, he does not spare him, that is, he does not avoid for him the burden which is the result of man's sin. And, positively, he makes of him the "instrument of purification" and the "locus of communion" in our regard (Rom. 8, 32; Jn. 3, 16; 6, 32; 1 Jn. 4, 9–10).

Jesus gives his life in a negative sense: he surrenders his earthly life as *a ransom;* and (positively) he communicates his risen life *as our food* (Mt. 20, 28; 26, 26; Gal. 2, 20; Tit. 2, 14; Jn. 6, 52. 56; 17, 19).

Jesus *gives his life for us.* Negatively, he willingly accepts death in a situation which corresponds with our sins (reestablishment of the faithful response and reparation of the scandal caused by sin). Positively, the blood which he sheds is the instrument of our purification, or, in other words, by accepting death Jesus passes into the state in which he can reconsecrate us to God.

He gives us his life positively while he lives on this earth: he shares our condition by spending in the service of men all his strength and every moment of his existence. Since his resurrection he makes us sharers of the life which he now lives.

But the redemption also comprises, on the part of men, the gift of self to God. More precisely, men make this gift of self in corresponding to the love of God.

Jesus gives himself to the Father: he does not give him a gift which he deprives himself of in order to make of it God's possession; he himself returns to God; he gives himself, with all his love, into God's hands. Through love for the Father he willingly leaves a situation in which there was in a way a lack of perfection in communion; he leaves it, in fact, to share the glorious life of the Father. There he receives the gift of the Father and there he gives himself to the Father, that is, he *lives in active communion,* in *reciprocal fidelity* (Jn. 10, 17; Lc. 23, 46; Heb. 9, 13–14).[1]

Accomplishing this gift of self in our name, Jesus draws us after him into communion with his Father (1 Pet. 3, 18). In Jesus and through Jesus we receive the vocation and the ability *to give ourselves to God.* The dialogue becomes more perfect because it is in union with Christ that we share in the life of love of the Father, the Son, and the Holy Spirit.

III. CONTINUATION

The work of the redemption continues because Christ himself is at work in his Church, to which he has communicated his Spirit, and because he summons us to labor with him in the Church.

The revelation concerning this continuance of the redemption is complete at the close of apostolic times. But the understanding of this revelation is still developing in *the growing consciousness* and *the practical application* of the different aspects presented by the union of Christ and his members.

[1] Cf. M. van Caster, "Self-Surrender to God at Mass," in *Lumen Vitae* IX (1954), pp. 36–45.

A. Pluralism in Types of Spirituality and Living

(a) After having traced in a genetic presentation three aspects of Christian mentality, we will attempt to show that they constitute the dialectical stages of a synthesis.

1. *Eschatological Spirituality*

On Pentecost the Church came into being through the advent of the Spirit sent by the risen Christ. Immediately the first Christians understood that they belonged, in some sense, to "the last ages". Christ had reached the immortal plenitude of salvation; he had ransomed those whom the Father had given him; they themselves had just received the messianic gift par excellence, namely, the Spirit of charity; they were soon to receive a share in the *"resurrection* of the flesh".

To do so they entered into the mystery of *the cross* by baptism, which made them pass into "union with Christ"; they renounced sin which was in the world; they made up in their own persons the Church of *the redeemed*. This is what they celebrated in *the liturgy;* it is this to which they gave living witness in the practice of charity and *detachment* from the goods of this world.

Even when it became clear that the Lord's return was not near, chronologically speaking, this spirituality remained "eschatological" in its confrontation with persecution. Martyrdom was the most splendid participation in the cross of Christ and gave immediate access to heaven.

The *deficiencies* of a spiritual outlook too exclusively concerned with eschatology were soon to become apparent, and they would give rise to new emphases.

2. *Spirituality of the Cross*

The experience of sin and of sinful tendencies, not done away with at a single stroke by baptism but requiring a real asceticism, drew attention to certain aspects of a "crucifying" spirituality which, up to that time, had remained in the shadows. These aspects, too, were to develop in a one-sided manner.

The first consideration was the fact that the Christian must struggle against the sin which is present within himself; he must do penance for the sins he has committed; he must mortify the tendencies that lead to sin. Next, penance and reparation were placed in the context of substitution or compensation: the innocent man accepts the role of suffering for the guilty. Finally, even apart from sin, suffering came to be considered as "merit" for heaven, and as "the price to be paid" for a fruitful apostolate. In the practice of this spirituality of the cross many Christians have given proof of great generosity and of a real love for Jesus Crucified.

But all one-sided development leads to a falsification of perspective, whether in practice, or in the theory in which an attempt is made to justify the habits that have been acquired. The defects in a one-sided spirituality of mortification are the following:

(1) the unorthodox elements in the interpretation given to the sacrifice of Jesus on the Cross (cf. preceding pages on this subject, as well as future sections in which we analyze the terms employed in the different interpretations);

(2) exaggerated or oversimplified statements on the value of suffering considered in itself (suffering has value only when endured in reference to something other than itself);

(3) a deviation in the direction of *moralism,* and,

consequently, an incorrect theory of grace, with, in practice, a false priority given to actual grace in order to protect sanctifying grace, which alone makes it possible to enter heaven.

There were elements of the Christian life that had not yet reached their full maturity. Therefore, the following type of spirituality should be considered rather as one more step (and not the last, see No. 4) in the maturation of Christian consciousness on the subject of the redemption.

3. *Spirituality of the Incarnation*

Here attention is directed principally to *the effects that grace*—and especially sanctifying grace—*operate in the whole man.* Now when one analyzes the relations between the natural and the supernatural, between man in his natural state and man in the state of grace, one proceeds simply along the line of theory, beginning with the entrance of the supernatural into the human sphere, notably through the incarnation of the Son of God.

It is, therefore, possible to say: God the Son, by becoming man, in principle sanctifies all that is human and even the whole of material creation. This sanctification in principle becomes a reality for each man at the moment of his baptism; it is increased by each action of the Christian that is accomplished in the state of grace. It gives to every Christian a superhuman dignity; it bestows this dignity even on every non-Christian, since he is really called to become a Christian. The Christian life is a Christian humanism, a superhumanism. It should embrace all things. This is the work of Christians in this world; it will reach its fullness in the plenitude of salvation, that is, in the condition of new men living on a new earth.

The cross and eschatological transcendence (more than human fulfillment) have not been denied in this point of view. But they are spoken of infrequently, if at all. Instead, the Christian must be ready to accept suffering in order to carry out his task of the Christian transformation of the world. But it is not up to him to withdraw from the world, quite the reverse. And here, by a play on words, which has not always been noted, we pass to *another sense of the word "incarnation":* the Christian must live "incarnate" and his apostolate must be "incarnate", for it is in this way that Christ will more and more be "incarnate" in the world.

The *defects* of this attitude stem from a double source. The first, and theoretic one, consists in a line of argument which considers only the "continuity" between nature and grace, even if the latter is understood as not rising out of nature, but coming down to nature from above. The second and existential defect consists in forgetting the "situation" in which the incarnation of Christ (in its primary sense) takes place, and the ulterior situation in which the "incarnation" (in its derived or secondary sense) of the Christian is to be effected in the world. Now in both cases what is real is the "redemption situation".

Let us compare the two possible interpretations of the term, "salvation by redemptive incarnation."

(1) In terms of the spirituality we have just been describing, the act by which the divine person of the Son unites himself to human nature has, *per se,* substantial redemptive value; the other acts are only complementary "accidents". The Christian would be saved by participating in this fundamental act of incarnation.

(2) According to the spirituality which we will examine (No. 4), the redemptive force of the incarnation

extends to the existential elements of the real situation of the Son of God made man. It entails, in fact, the redemptive action which consists in the passage through death to resurrection, an action carried out by the Son of God Incarnate.

Henceforth, the "real" Christian is he who participates in this unique existential "way" of the redemption, which passes through the cross and leads to heaven. This real and final end consists in a transformation that is not simply the effect of the Christian's action on the world. This reminder of the end, brings us back to the importance of the essential "eschatological" component of all Christian spirituality. And from it emerges a quite remarkable fact: the genetic development of the growth of consciousness we have just traced, and the synthesis of the three essential "dialectical phases" we are going to describe, proceed, with respect to one another, in opposite directions.

4. Spirituality of the Redemption: a Synthesis of the Three Preceding Types or Viewpoints

The mentality and the attitude that characterize this spirituality may be summed up in terms of *participation in the existential "way" of Christ:* man walks the roads of this life going in the same direction and acting in the same way as Christ who has gone before us and draws us after him. There is a real sharing and a real difference between Christ and us. A real participation, not only in imitating his exterior actions, but also by union with the interior dispositions of Christ.

There are real differences: first of all, Christ came of his own free will to share our human situation; we are plunged into it without having willed it, but it is up to us willingly to assume our role in this situation. Again, the participation of Christ did not make of him a sinner;

but every man bears during his whole life first the interior effects of original sin, and then, for each personal sin he needs once more God's pardon for himself. From these facts emerge the following three "dialectical moments" or phases:

(a) *We must accept our complex situation, a situation that needs redemption and in which redemption is going on; and with it we must accept the role that God assigns to us.*

The components of our existential situation are not at first glance clear to us. Therefore, our acceptance begins by being global: "Our Father . . . thy will be done." And in the degree to which the elements of the situation become clearer to us, we are called upon to give a more explicit acquiescence, sometimes even a public witness to our acceptance of the entire "Christian condition".

Jesus has gone before us in this acceptance: he has done so in his human life with its domestic and temporal tasks at Nazareth; in the special illumination on his role in the service of the Father at Jerusalem; in the official acceptance of that role in a sinful world, on the banks of the Jordan.

At the time of our baptism—when the adult accepts the Christian condition (see page 43f.)—we receive *the grace* for the initial assumption as a Christian of the components of our situation: first, we are called to live supernaturally united to God in Christ Jesus, and to do so in such a way that our tasks in this world— especially our relations with our neighbor—will be animated with supernatural charity. Hence, the necessity to unite to our normal concern for these temporal commitments a real detachment which is one form of our confidence in God. Secondly, we must accept the active presence of sin, in the world and in ourselves. Hence the necessity for struggle taking the form of carrying our cross, but a struggle whose happy issue is ensured by God in virtue of our union with Christ.

It is not enough *to receive this good news with joy*, namely, that Christ's redemption is operative in our personal lives, and to accept this struggle *in principle*. We must also show ourselves faithful. This is the second of the dialectical moments.

(b) *We must witness to our fidelity to grace in trial.*

The "good news" soon shows that it does not, purely and simply, satisfy our instinctive yearnings. Nor does it satisfy the tendency of our minds to judge all things by the light of reason and to reject what goes beyond their natural powers.

Life lived according to the Gospel demands a continuing conversion. It also demands constancy in the trials coming from "the world". In other words, the difficulty we experience in living the Christian life is inherent in our existential situation. The cross, which most closely resembles the cross of Christ, consists in the suffering caused by men who are opposed to the good we seek to do and to the truth we seek to proclaim. When this cross looms up on the horizon of our lives, it remains for us—as it was for Peter when Jesus announced it—a scandal and a temptation to revolt and discouragement. This temptation assails us even when we personally are spared, as when, in the historical process, the good seems to be nailed to the cross by evil, blow by blow. On the other hand, it is enough for us to have some human success, or simply that the tenets of "integral humanism", with God left out of account, be preached, and our fidelity to humble dependence on God's grace be questionable.

Jesus saved us by remaining faithful to the love of God and of men, and in particular by remaining faithful to confidence in his Father in the darkness of the final trial. The spirituality of participation in the action of the redemption implies fidelity that is not simply *moral,* that is, concerned with observance, but above all *spiritual,* that is, trust in God's help. And this remains true even after painful experience of the sin of personal infidelity, even when the effort of the whole Church seems so painfully slow in bringing about the victory of truth and charity.

When fidelity like this is to be reached it has a sacramental dimension, and in particular a eucharistic dimension. In participating in *the sacrifice of the mass,* the Christian sincerely desires to be faithful-with-Jesus in every trial. And the grace of the eucharist communicates to him a growing strength so to be.

This fidelity must have its *public witness,* not only in the liturgical celebration, but in every Christian practice. Then it constitutes, in its union with the public witness of Jesus on the cross, the reparation for the scandal caused by sin. As in the case of Jesus, this witness receives its complement in a manifestation of the resurrection.

(c) *We must anticipate and prepare for the realization of eschatological values.*

It is from the vantage point of his faith in eschatological values, *already realized in the person of Jesus the redeemer,* that the Christian structures his own value system and that he directs his efforts toward realization in this world. The "spirituality of the redemption" appreciates first of all the possible *anticipation* of personalist values considered in their eschatological dimension, notably communion with God, shared by the Christian community in its union with the risen Christ present in *the eucharistic celebration.*

Another participation is to be found in the practice of the evangelical counsels.

This same spirituality considers every human task to be accomplished in the setting of this world as so many real *acts of preparation,* "rough drafts" of eternal life. Action in this world, carried out in the perspective of faith and with the charity of Christ, is never reduced to the level of a purely human means which may be thrown away once the end has been reached. Man's acts in time transform the man himself, and this result is taken up into the eschatological situation in a transcendant manner.

The parable "contains" in some sense what is beyond it; but the parable will give way to what it imperfectly means; the meaning glimpsed by the parable will be realized to perfection. Thus, temporal values are, for the Christian, so many "intermediate ends"; he places on them *an entirely realistic and "open" price,* which is lower than the values, in eschatological terms, toward which they tend.

Therefore, in this relationship of the three phases of the spirituality of the redemption—incarnation, the cross and the resurrection—are to be found the outlines of the very *movement* of the paschal mystery. It is for this reason that we may call this viewpoint *a paschal spirituality.*

(b) The diversity of these types of spirituality presents certain *analogies* which we do not wish to exaggerate, but which nonetheless deserve our attention as a matter of catechesis.

1. *Types of Spirituality and Their Relationship to Psychological Development*

What concerns us here is the affinity of certain aspects

of spirituality with psychological sensibility. Catechetical method must at one and the same time correspond to this sensibility and be alert to remedy its defects.

Before the age of 9, *the child* is very sensitive to the promise of heaven, for he lives secure in the protection of God our Father, and he experiences both curiosity and desire to see how we will be "at home" in the Father's house. Knowledge of religious truths and the attitude toward them are still somewhat vague. An eschatological spirituality will meet no resistance so long as neither the "distance" caused by sin nor the attachment to this world can claim the innocent conscience. From these facts arises the difficulty, at this age, of understanding the meaning of redemption by the cross.

But the age of *social and legal conformity* (ages 9 to 12) and *the age when one desires to realize by one's own strength an ideal conceived as belonging to one's own personality* (ages 13 to 15) bring with them also the sense of distance between what is to be done and what has in reality been accomplished. Hence the sensitivity, at this period, to penance and to mortification, as counterweights to legal and moral deficiencies; hence also, by way of prolongation and ambiguous complement, the appeal of an effort at mortification conceived as imitation of Christ on the cross.

At the same time—and this is the second reason why the eschatological spirituality fades into the background —the discovery of the world and the attraction of human values practically absorb all the attention.

This interest is transformed into a challenge to commitment when adolescence is replaced by *youth* (ages 16 to 24). It is a deeply felt challenge to the realization of human relations (love) and to the re-making of the world (by professional action) on the one hand, accompanied by a (temporary) lack of experience of the difficulties of the real world, on the other. It follows that among these young people—and we are not here speaking of those who mean that there is no access to life lived in all its fullness—among these young people, full of enthusiasm for the future, there is a special sensibility to a spirituality of the incarnation that does not take into account the necessities of the redemption.

Only in *maturity* is it possible to unite in all their significance the components that have successively been engaging our attention. The adult lives in the real world; he feels that this reality is the battlefield of divine and human forces, of good and evil tendencies, of inertia and progressive energy, of failure and of humble renewals founded in God. He knows at least a little about history, with its constants of human conduct and special interventions on the part of God. He believes that human life rests on the life of Jesus Christ. He knows that nothing can be built up as it should be, until it has been properly "saved"; that no tendency is fully Christian unless it unites active gratitude for the gift of God which is to bear fruit, with the characteristic detachment of "the poor of Yahweh". He knows that all effort toward the good is sure to encounter the cross; he knows that no really profound human problem will be fully solved on this earth.

Participating in the existential "way" of Christ, he recognizes it more and more perfectly in faith, and, in the light of faith, he commits himself to *"the Church on her way"* that is, to the Pilgrim Church on her journey toward that final acceptance of the supreme surprise which God reserves for us in the total encounter with Christ.

Is it necessary to note that the psychological development we have in mind is not merely a matter of biological stages? We are here dealing with *psychological periods*. If there are people with psychological reactions lagging behind their biological development, there are others and even children who give signs of an advanced spiritual maturity.

In the same way, when we speak of a "manner of life" it will be good to recall the fact that we have in mind a "mentality": it is possible for a layman in the world to have a larger share of "religious mentality" than a man who has made profession of the religious vows but who has only a very limited degree of eschatological mentality.

2. *Spirituality and Manner of Life*

Elsewhere we have shown how the life of *a religious man* or woman emphasizes the eschatological aspect of Christianity, and how the life of *the Christian in the world* emphasizes aspects of the incarnation understood as a "consecration" of terrestrial human values. All exclusivism leads us outside truth and reality: the religious is still a real part of this world, and the Christian cannot collaborate in a real consecration unless he is sufficiently receptive to the eschatological dimension—to detachment through death and "surpassing" into different form—which Christian consecration supposes.

Nevertheless, there is a difference between the two spiritualities. And it must be evident even when the religious and the Christian in the world are engaged in the same work. For example, it is possible for them to collaborate in Christian education, to give the same courses, to aim at the same type of Christian, to care for the same sick, but the motives of the work and the witness they will give in carrying it out will have different nuances.

Once again the incarnation and eschatology bring us face to face with the necessity for a synthesis based on the redemption, a synthesis which will be explicitly related to the fact of sin and which cannot be understood except by considering the work of Christ in its entirety.

B. Liturgical Celebrations

Our considerations turn now to the relationship existing between the liturgy and the continuation of the mystery of the redemption.

1. *Unity of the Three Aspects of the Mystery*

The mystery of salvation is a mystery of an "economy" realized within an historical setting.[2] The economy of salvation consists in the inter-personal relationship that God establishes and reestablishes between men and himself in Christ Jesus. This economy also includes the various modes of action he selects in order to cement this relationship. And among these processes, the liturgical celebrations have a privileged position.

The encounter between God and man in Jesus Christ takes place first of all in certain historical events, notably in the cross and resurrection which form the center of the history of redemption. But in these events it is an action of supra-historical dimensions which God realizes. This supra-historical and salvific action can be made present in the symbolical actions of the established cult, namely, in the liturgical celebrations.

It is for this reason that the whole of the Christian liturgy bears a fundamental relationship to the cross-and-resurrection of Jesus. By itself this event is the cen-

[2] M. van Caster, *The Structure of Catechetics, Chap.* II, (New York: Herder and Herder, 1965).

ter of a history, and the events of every human life are also intended to become elements of this history. Therefore, the liturgy can never be divorced from Christian charity made actual in life and work outside of worship proper. Hence, there is an essential bond between *the existential aspect*—the life of Jesus and the life of the Christian—and *the liturgical aspect* of the mystery.

Now every relation destined to be lived by persons requires to be known: men must at least have a certain consciousness of the meaning of the mystery of salvation, that is, there also exists an essential connection or a relationship uniting the events, the rites and the manner in which the mystery is understood: this is *the doctrinal aspect*. We will point out later certain nuances related to this subject.

Because of this double connection and by reason of their own validity, liturgical celebrations have a privileged position in the continuation of the mystery of the redemption within the Church. These celebrations are of various kinds. We cannot here embark upon an exposition of the special meaning of each one, for it would be necessary to show how each one is related to the mystery of the cross and the resurrection. We will here limit ourselves to the two sacraments in which the connection we have spoken of is most luminous.

2. *Baptism: the Initial Celebration of the Redemption*

The existential reality of the redemption consists in a communion of charity, but, as a result of sin, this communion is made conditional on purification. Redemption is a "passage" from the state of sin, with all its consequences, to the state of charity, with its consequences, namely, to the life of active charity.

Baptism is the passage from the state of sin, which brings with it separation, impotence, death and the need for purification, to the state of communion, which is established by a "belonging" both given and accepted, and which requires to be lived and developed in all its fullness.

The symbols of baptism are related to rites of passage envisioning a new life, a new beginning.

Thus, the passage through the Red Sea, renewed in the crossing of the Jordan, manifests the deliverance from slavery in a foreign land and the entering into, or the new beginning in, liberty in the land of "peace". In subsequent ages, a deliverance of another kind became more manifestly necessary: the deliverance which is purification from sin in order to take part in the messianic expectations. This is the reason why John the Baptist comes to the Jordan to confer the baptism of penance.

It is highly significant that the Evangelists place "the beginning of the public life" in the same context, and it is not without an explicit intention that they do so. At this same place on the banks of the Jordan Jesus takes his position as the leader of the new people of God, for the entrance into the promised land, and that he accepts its onerous condition of participation in the human lot (see page 19). This conscious and public initiative is, therefore, directed toward the "hour" of plenary redemption. And in realizing in his own person, as Head of the human race, the passage to the undying fullness of salvation, Jesus declares by what sacramental sign men can and must effectively set out following him: baptism.

The sign of the water and the words point to *a passage which is a purification and a new beginning*. This sign and these words are to be understood in the entire context of salvation history, especially in that of the baptism of Jesus and, above all, in the context of his cross and resurrection. They have their efficacy in the power Jesus exercises to make men sharers in the redemption he effects.

Therefore, the reality of baptism, signified in its symbolic action, can be described as follows: the man in sin receives, by hearing the words of Christ, the light that makes him know that salvation is communicated in the name of Christ in and by the Church. Therefore, he presents himself to the Church to be baptized. By his incorporation in Christ and in virtue of his participation in the cross and resurrection of Christ, this man passes from sin into the friendship of God, from death to a new life in union with Jesus Christ, from the world—that is, from the milieu controlled by the devil—to the Christian community of the Church, the milieu in which the action of the Holy Spirit is sacramentally and effectively exercised.

As with everything that belongs to the mystery of the redemption, the baptismal action is a cooperation between God and man, in Christ Jesus. It is God who takes the initiative; it is God who "translates" (Col. 1, 13) man from one existential situation to another. As for man, his role is humbly to accept God's saving action, and, by "being converted" to commit himself with confidence into God's hands to live according to the situation in which the Lord has placed him.

What is proper to baptism is its character of *"initial" sacramental celebration.* The passage (which will remain characteristic and will have to be carried out again in a different way throughout the whole of the Christian's life) is a real and even a radical one in baptism; but it is still only a beginning. Baptismal catechesis must insist on these two aspects: (1) a real purification has already taken place, a real participation in the Christ-life, a real membership in the Church; (2) but, all this is true in such a way that it must constantly be renewed with different modalities and following the call to progress in perfection.

Purification, even if it remits all sin, has not, for all that, broken the many bonds with tendencies toward sin; the new life is held only in the hands of a weak creature, an infant; and membership in the Church, while it is definitive from many points of view, is still exposed to many vicissitudes. In the varied and progressive renewals of this "passage" by which we share in the redemption, every liturgical celebration has its part to play. In this sense, one of the effects of baptism, to which attention should especially be drawn, is the fact that it makes us capable of participating in the other sacraments, and above all of acting more fully with Jesus Christ in the eucharist.

3. The Eucharist, the Principal Celebration of the Redemption

When we spoke of the relation of the three aspects of the mystery (see No. 1), we reserved the question of the nuances of the doctrinal aspect for later consideration. We use this term here in a wider sense than a "doctrine defined by faith". We intend to speak of every manner of reflecting on revealed truths, and of the different and valid ways of placing emphasis on them. Thus we advert to what we have said about the pluralism of types of spirituality, and we note that the way of understanding and emphasizing the connection between the eucharist and the redemption will vary with the influence of these various types.

(a) First, *eschatological spirituality:* the primitive

Church celebrated the eucharist as *a meal taken with the risen Christ.* If this celebration also proclaimed the death of Christ, it did so in the consciousness that the Christ of the New Pasch had conquered death and that the Christians were preparing themselves for full participation in his triumph.

The emphasis was also on the *"spiritual" cult,* that is, "living", "existential", and especially on *fraternal charity* based on the love of God and detachment from earthly goods. The eucharistic meal has a well-defined fraternal dimension. As for the ritual dimension, it is as yet very little developed.

When a certain nostalgia for the rich ceremonial of the Temple was felt by some of the faithful, the author of the Epistle to the Hebrews does not counter it by fixing attention on the eucharistic celebration, but by recalling the unique significance and perfect fulfillment of the (existential) sacrifice of the cross, a significance he expresses analogically in ritual terms.

This is the place for an important observation. In virtue of the bond between the existential aspect and the liturgical aspect of the mystery (see page 42), the existential reality can be expressed in ritual terms, and the ritual actions can signify the existential reality that gives them value. Now the liturgy has a tendency to say what it is doing ritually, and, in this way, to employ expressions fitting for "things". Thus, in the sacrifice, words will be used that describe and explain actions done with things: "Receive, O holy Father, this host . . . this sacrifice." It is important always to inject a personalist sense into these expressions, and with it the spiritual sacrifice which is the free gift of self. This observation is particularly applicable to the concept of the eucharist adopted in the following type of spirituality.

(b) Experience of the persistence of sin and of the necessity of penance gives rise to *the spirituality of the cross.* Those who put the accent on a renewed reparation due to God for sin, see in the mass *the means of offering Christ as a victim of reparation.* But in the use of these terms we detect a twofold tendency. First, there is the tendency which we have just noted in connection with treating personalist actions as if they were "things". Secondly, there is some ambiguity in the use of the word *victim.*

Originally, and quite correctly, the word signified the being which becomes *sacred* in the sacrifice (*sacrum facere*). Christ is, therefore, a victim in a personalist manner as he freely carries out the action of the sacred return to the Father (Jn. 19, 17). But from the fact that the sacrifice often involves death, the word *victim* is taken to indicate a being that meets with a disagreeable fate, specifically with suffering and death.

We have already noted that the theory which would see in Christ a suffering victim, undergoing chastisement, and paying the ransom exacted by justice, is exposed to grave distortions. The same thing is also true, *a fortiori,* for a theory which would see in the mass the oblation (as of a thing) of a (suffering?) victim. What is valid in the concept of Chirst as a victim of the cross and in the mass will find a more suitable context in a spirituality of the resurrection.

This spirituality also develops another aspect based on the necessity for penance and mortification. Taking part in the mass becomes in a special way *the giving to God, in union with the death of Jesus Christ, of our sacrifices,* our privations and penances. To receive holy communion is to receive the grace to be transformed into Jesus crucified, so as to be able at some future date to share in his triumph.

(c) Another type of spirituality, without denying the fact of sin and all its consequences, holds that the direct end of every act of worship is to give glory to God, and that this is done most directly by praise. This *spirituality of praise* gives rise to such expressions as *sacrifice of praise*. But this term can be understood in a number of different ways: is it the ritual sacrifice which constitutes the praise? does the ritual sacrifice deserve praise because it expresses sincere religious attitudes? or is it the prayer of praise which is said, by analogy, to be a sacrifice, a sacrifice which consists in offering up prayers? With persons who are especially devoted to prayer, this last meaning is preferred. In the mass the accent is then placed on the *"thanksgiving"* (the *eucharistia*), which is, more or less exactly, the equivalent of *praise, adoration, blessing.*

Christians unite themselves to *Jesus, the Priest and Adorer*. Since Holy Scripture reminds us that Christ in heaven is ever living to make intercession for us (Heb. 7, 25), the sacrifice of the mass is understood more precisely as a participation in the state of eternal oblation in which Christ is living in heaven. And the grace of the eucharist is to make of men, Christians whose whole life is in a certain sense a prolongation of the eucharistic praise.

(d) But in fact this perpetual praise is understood by others in such a way as, without excluding anything, would reverse the position of the elements of human prayer-activity in the world. The *spirituality of the incarnation* (second meaning, see page 33) considers, in fact, that all human activity in which Christian charity becomes "incarnate" is, by analogy, a prayer in contact with God and made to God's glory. For those who place the accent on the consecration of the world by the action of Christians, the mass becomes the liturgy of the oblation of Christian realizations. It is then the center for worship, *the place where Christians come in union with the sacrifice of Christ to offer their labor,* their suffering, their joy, their success and their failures.

This is done in a sense, not always very precise, in an attitude that contains some profoundly worthwhile elements, but also, at times, without perceiving that the emphasis has been shifted from the sacrifice of Christ (in which we should take part) to the sacrifices of men, upon which the sacrifice of Christ confers a special efficacy. In this theory it is usual to overlook the fact that these actions and these activist attitudes, which we bring as our offering, always need to be purified. To reach a more balanced synthesis, it seems to us that it is important to shed light once again on the whole picture of biblical data, which concerns at one and the same time the eucharist and the whole mystery of the redemption.

(e) A better understanding of the relation existing between the redemption and the eucharist is, providentially, favored in our own day by two striking features of thought and action within the Church: namely, the return to biblical sources and the communal sense of the mystical body of Christ.

Hence, *the spirituality of the redemption* has today *a paschal and communal character,* and the eucharist is seen to occupy a central position as the principal liturgical *participation* by way of prayer and of sacramental action in the paschal "passage", that is, in *the existential "way" of the crucified and risen Christ.* This participation in the eucharist makes for growth in *love* among all those who are called to live in communion with the Father, the Son, and the Holy Spirit.

For further explanation, see (*infra*) the analytical section and the catechetical conclusions (pp. 83, 102).

4. *The Liturgical Year, the Unfolding of the Redemption*

The structure of the liturgical year corresponds to a double movement: one goes from the center to the periphery, the other, from the periphery to the center. The center, which holds the mystery in its totality, is the cross-and-resurrection of the Son of God made man, and the riches of this mystery require it to be unfolded in its many aspects. From another point of view, the central celebration, in order to give its full worth, must be prepared; it must also be extended in its effects; this second aspect constitutes the movement from the periphery to the center and back again.

In this continuous dynamism of the same mystery are to be recognized the principal and distinct "moments". In each phase the Church proclaims one aspect of the revelation so that we may be conscious of a call originating in one of God's gifts, and she awakens within us a *sense* of the spiritual attitude which is called for in response.

(a) *Paschal Cycle*

Consciousness of the divine origins of our life. God's call. Sense of the task to which we have been summoned: *Septuagesima*.

Consciousness of the need of redemption. Sense of sin. Reminder of the riches we have received and of the duties assumed in baptism. Penance for our sins: *Lent*.

Consciousness of the reality of the sufferings and death of Jesus, without suppressing the unity of the paschal mystery, since the resurrection is always in the the background. Sense of the necessity to remain faithful in our trials: *Passiontide*.

Consciousness of the triumphant life of Christ. Sense

of our participation in his life: *Resurrection and Ascension*.

Consciousness of the effects of the redemption: the gift of the Spirit. Sense of the need for spiritual growth and of the apostolate: *Pentecost*.

Consciousness of the fulfillment of the promise. Sense of active orientation toward the parousia.

(b) *Epiphany Cycle*

The redemption is a transcendant and invisible mystery made visible and accessible by its signs.

The epiphany—*showing-forth*—of God in deeds of strength, goodness and redemptive fidelity. Manifestation of the fidelity of Christ in his humanity. Sense of faith in the invisible through the visible mediation.

(c) *The Sanctoral Cycle*

The saints have shared and still share in an eminent manner in the union of Christ and his members in the work of redemption.

Among them *Mary* has a special role, so that special mention is made of her even in the cycles that unfold the mystery of Christ himself. The 1963 *Constitution on the Liturgy* (cf. Arts. 103, 104) has made definite statements on both these subjects.

C. Structure, Means, Results

1. *Diversity of Functions*

(a) The functions of the hierarchy are the instrumental continuation of the functions of the Head; they are the functions belonging to Christ, notably, those he has as the one invested by the Father with power to redeem, and as the one who represents all the people of God.

Through *the ministry of the Word* in the Church, Jesus continues to call sinners to repentance and to deliverance from ignorance by revealing to them the Father's designs for salvation.

By *the ministry of the sacraments,* Christ the redeemer continues to forgive sins and to communicate his own life.

Priests who exercise these ministries are the instruments of the continuing redemptive action of God himself. They are the executors of the one Christian priesthood, namely that of Christ himself.

In *the liturgical prayer* addressed to God, above all in the eucharist, they are also the bearers, with Christ and in the name of the whole people, of man's response to God. We will speak of this when we discuss the union of the sacerdotal ministry with the faithful (pp. 53f., 91).

(b) As for the functions of the members, in the first place, they concern essentially the "response" to be given by men. For sinners, the first requirement is a heart opened to hearing the call to conversion addressed to them by Christ. After this, our collaboration is shown by our repentance, our plea for forgiveness, and by the mortification of our disordered passions. The strength to perfect this conversion is given to us by our meeting with God in the sacraments.

This first step will be followed by an indefinite number of others, in which our "conversion" is continued and we live, in terms of our re-established fidelity, in union with Christ. The fidelity of our charity will have a special value for reparation if we are obliged to practice it in trial (see page 54f.). The witness of this fidelity will be a reparation for the evil done by scandal. And the best reparation for a bad influence consists, certainly, in the good influence we may exercise in the apostolate.

Indeed, as soon as we have ceased refusing ourselves to God when, not only does he reconcile us with himself, but he entrusts to us a mission of influence: Christians *have to act for God* in the world. Every act in which the members of the Church share in her apostolate has, in Christ, co-redemptive value.

But here, too, there is room for a vast number of different modalities.

A very special role was entrusted by God to Mary, the Mother of Jesus. She is the prototype of the Church in her receptivity of the redemption effected by Christ, and in her active participation in the extension of the redemption by the prayer of intercession and the witness of her life. And she exercises this maternal role with respect to all men.

Regarding the *fraternal members* of the Church, we must here be satisfied with noting the great diversity of particular vocations without going into the consequences in detail: religious life and life in the world; contemplatives, "penitents", and active religious; the laity, married and single, etc. For each category it will be necessary to note the proper characteristics, but these are secondary by comparison with the common and fundamental task incumbent on all members of the Church.

2. *Unity of prayer, of apostolate and of Redemptive fidelity in trial*

The collaboration of all, each according to his function, in the continuation of the redemptive work of Christ himself, is most central and most clearly manifest in the communal celebration of the eucharist (see page 84).

The sincerity of our active participation in the liturgy demands *a many-sided commitment in everyday life.* We will simply note here three forms:

(a) Any service rendered to our neighbor, and all inter-personal relations in the community: the practice of charity develops salvation itself, which consists in love.

(b) Fidelity in trial: each trial can be accepted by the Christian in union with Christ, in a spirit of expiation, either as personal mortification or as communal reparation;

(c) The apostolate: every good influence works for the restoration of the kingdom of heaven.

But there is a combination of all three forms which deserves a more extended examination in view of its special redemptive value: it is fidelity in trial when it stems directly from the works of the apostolate (see pp. 92, 122).

Our participation is more determined according to the relationship that exists between religious redemption and the temporal liberation of man as the object of the work of redemption.

3. *Objectives and Results*

The question of the relationship between redemption in the religious sense and temporal liberation, or in more positive terms, between Christian salvation and human development, is as vast and complex as the question of the entire mission which the Church must progressively carry out through her priests and the faithful. The point of view from which we will briefly consider it here is that of the Christian redemption in its genetic presentation

At the moment of the Exodus the redemption wrought

by God and the human liberation of the Hebrews were one and the same. Subsequently, the need for deliverance from sin came to the fore, and, in a positive sense, union with God is what corresponds to it. Finally, Christ reveals the existence of two stages in its realization. The fullness of salvation, of which his miracles are the first signs, is reserved not for earth and time, but for another setting. The work of redemption, which is to be carried out on earth and in the course of human history, requires in the first place a religious and moral *conversion,* then *a growth in union with God* which is especially shown in *love for one's neighbor*.

This charity becomes "incarnate", successively and in many ways, in cultural and social transformations. The world of matter and the technical progress of men remains, nonetheless, always ambiguous. Therefore, the attention given to the struggle against sin and *the concern for conversion* even in our concept of progress are always present and needful. All religious progress and *the progressive "incarnation" of charity in the world* is a preparation for the eschatological fulfillment of man and of the world which is to be awaited as a special gift from God (see page 94).

As *conclusion* and as the first *synthesis* of the entire genetic presentation, it is clear that *the history of redemption is the history of a fidelity that triumphs over infidelity*.

Out of love God created man to respond to love and to live in communion with him. When, by his refusal, that is, by his *infidelity,* man plunged into the miserable and scandalous condition of sin, it is *first of all the fidelity of God* that comes into play and will remain the principal agent of the redemption. God is faithful to the merciful love he has for man. This is the reason why he sends us his Son, invested with power to save and ready to exercise that power in conditions that are at once most appropriate to our humanity and most difficult to himself because of our hardness of heart.

In its turn, *the fidelity of the Son of God made man* is shown in an efficacious manner. Jesus is faithful to act *for* his Father with regard to us, and *for* us before God. He shows his faithful love, which is obedience to the Father and the service of men, in the most extreme trials in which all our sins weigh most heavily. It is for this reason that the fidelity of Christ re-establishes humanity in the true response to the love of God, delivers us and makes reparation for the scandal of sin.

In the same way in which he responded in our name to every demand, Christ himself is the first to receive, in the name of the whole human race, the immortal and glorious perfection of salvation.

In the grace of the Holy Spirit, which the risen Christ communicates to us, *our growing fidelity* is directed to total and final communion.

Charity remains always faithful to itself, and it remains forever. God is charity. The redemption of those who had refused charity-by-love is accomplished by the faithful love of the Son of God, the perfect mediator, and by our active participation in his cross and resurrection; a participation which makes us increasingly receptive to his action in us, helps us in the constant struggle against sin, renders us capable to radiate his love so that all will be transformed by it.

CHAPTER II

ANALYSIS AND COMMENTARY

Biblical tradition and the tradition of the Church express the dogma of the redemption in a wide variety of terms. Some of these terms are more highly charged with personalist values; others make more of an appeal to materialistic or juridical analogies and need to be interpreted in a personalist and religious sense. It is with this end in view that we here analyze the terms most frequently employed.

1. *Redemption by Means of a Victorious Battle*

The image has reference to an action by means of which one person liberates another, either from bodily and social captivity, or from some other difficult situation: it is an act of "buying back" or ransom. When the liberator takes upon himself the difficulty of the action, we say that he "pays the ransom".

In the Bible, redemption is always an action of power and goodness. Therefore, the redeemer is he in whom the unfortunate man can put his trust: his *Go'ël* (he who has the power to save and who wills to do so) lives.

God, the mediators of the Old Testament, Jesus Christ—these are redeemers by analogy. Of all of them, the Bible says that they pay *a ransom*. But the value of the image stops there: to buy back is to pay a ransom, that is, to save by carrying out a difficult work; there is never any question of one *to whom* the ransom is paid. In particular, we never read that Jesus pays a ransom for us to his Father, as if he had to buy us out of a captivity in which God was keeping us; on the contrary, when he pays the ransom in his role as the perfect mediator, he purchases a people for his Father (Acts 20, 28).

The image of the ransom does not, therefore, indicate a creditor, but rather the onerous conditions in which the act of purchase—or the liberation—is effected. *Jesus* bears the full brunt of the difficulties which belong to the condition of sinful humanity, which he joins of his own free will without in any way sharing the guilt of sin. He comes to make manifest the love of the Father, and he comes to make a response in love and obedience, in difficult circumstances: this is the "ransom" which he pays. The sufferings which he meets with in these difficulties possess a passive and an active quality: Jesus has not sought these sufferings; they stem from his participation in our sinful human condition; but he freely wills not to avoid or evade them; it is of his own free will that he accepts what the Father asks of him, namely, that he will give his testimony as a mediator in the conditions that arise from our sins.

If the image of re-purchase must not be attached to the idea of a creditor, it can, on the other hand, be assimilated to the image of the warrior. Throughout the Bible, God appears as one who does battle for Israel against the enemies of his people who are his enemies. The mediators he sends lead this battle in his name. The ransom attached to their mission consists in a special manner in the burden of this *struggle*. And, as for other symbols, the significance of this one also becomes more interior. First, because it shows that the enemy is within the nation itself: it is the infidelity of the people; and then, because this enemy can only be overcome by obedience to God.

Moreover, this theme of struggle is crystallized in the combat between life and death. Through the Old and the New Testament all that is alive is attached to God, and, conversely, what is united to God, lives. In the same way, the Bible always sees united, often in a way that shows little differentiation, death (as man experiences it) and sin. Thus, the entire mystery of the redemption is presented as a struggle between God who makes man live, and the forces of sin which cause his death. Sin and death are considered as the powers of God's enemy: the devil.

The redeemer-mediator sent by God carries on this struggle in the strength of God and in fidelity to his mission. It is in this epic terminology of a struggle to the death between opposing powers that St. Paul presents the mystery of the redemption. The Father has sent his Son as mediator in this "encounter" between life and death. The obedience of Jesus is victorious over the disobedience of men. Triumphing over what is the cause of death, it robs death of its power; it develops into a new life which is life eternal.

In the terminology of combat, Jesus must come to grips with death itself in order to secure the triumph of life. Obedient even unto death, it is by his union with the living God that he snatches this victory from sin in the very domain where sin is powerful. In this sense we are to understand the declaration of Scripture that the Messiah "ought" to suffer and die in order to enter into life, for the Father had chosen this arena as the most suitable place for his Son to win the final victory over death, as much for his incarnate Son as for us. In the real context is to be found an important element that gives the following special meaning to the "necessity": the last of God's special envoys had to expect extreme opposition from men who did not want to accept his message.

In this perspective death is not, therefore, considered as a source of "merit" to be rewarded by some good external to the action performed and to its direct significance. Nor is it a prize due in justice, after the manner in which damages are awarded among men. But it is presented to us as the great enemy to be overcome so that life may triumph, and the acceptance of death finds its meaning in the obedience sustained by the Father's power, and overcomes sin on its own ground. In other words, according to scriptural terminology redemption does not present itself to us in commercial or juridical terms, but rather in epic terms. We will see shortly that this same reality can be presented in ritual terms.

2. Expiation-Purification

In the Bible the term *expiation* does not refer in the first instance to a chastisement, to some kind of punishment which is undergone, but rather to a divine intervention that has as its final effect *purification*.

When a man (or a group of men) has put himself into a state of impurity, whether by a voluntary transgression or by an involuntary failing, this state can be removed by a rite which has the force of purification. This force of purification comes from God himself. The principal rite of purification is the one which is accomplished by *the sprinkling with blood*. In fact, blood, being "sacred", has the power to "reunite" man to God. God has given blood for purification (Lev. 17, 11); that is, although all shedding of blood is forbidden because the blood—life—belongs to God, for the same reason the ritual sprinkling with blood permitted by God has the power to purify and consecrate (on the role of the blood, see page 74ff.).

On *the great day of purification and expiation* the Jews thank Yahweh for having given then the instrument of purification they need.[1]

Purification (coming from God) and petition for forgiveness, or *intercession for another* (coming from men) have their point of intersection in the liturgy. Therefore, the term to *intercede* as employed for the priest's action, sometimes means *to accomplish the rite of purification.* In the same way, the term *asham,* which is translated into Greek by a word which also signifies a sinful voluntary action, means first of all *the state* of guilt as a result of transgression whether voluntary or not, whether individual or collective, and it can also be used to designate *the sacrifice* of guilt, or, the ritual sacrifice in which the victim is the instrument for the forgiveness of sins.

By the gift of the "instrument of purification" and by the acceptance of the sacrifice in which the purification is effected, God shows himself propitious to men. Whence arise the terms "instrument of propitiation" and "sacrifice of propitiation".

The sprinkling takes place on the "propitiatory", the golden table placed above the Ark of the Covenant within the Holy of Holies. This is considered the throne

[1] S. Ligier, "Autour du sacrifice eucharistique," in *Nouvelle Revue théologique* 82 (1960), p. 47.

of Yahweh himself, where he is propitious, or where he manifests his propitiation.

In this context, it is the priest who "expiates"; he does not pay the penalty in the place of the guilty, but he "intercedes", that is, he implores and he carries out the rite which applies the "means of purification" in favor of the guilty one.

The Septuagint sometimes translates the Hebrew word signifying *means of purification* by the very same term that designates *means of ransom,* namely, the Greek term *lutron,* an instrument which unbinds.

All these terms are to be found in the New Testament to show how Jesus fulfills in a transcendant manner everything prepared in the Old Testament. They express the mission the Father entrusted to Christ, and the perfect charity with which Christ accomplished that mission. The Father made his Son "instrument of propitiation" (Rom. 3, 25). He sent him in the form of "sinful flesh" (in participation of the condition of sin, not in accord with willful sin, nor as a substitute for sinners) so that he could give his blood to purify men. The Father made him (the Son)—not "sin", as most translations assert—but *asham,* that is, the sacrifice for guilt, the sacrifice of propitiation (2 Cor. 5, 21).

Jesus carries out this mission with entire fidelity. His blood is not considered indebtedness exacted by the Father, but as the very gift of the Father which makes it into an instrument of deliverance (*lutron*), in a sacrifice that is also intercession—so that the Father will forgive us—but which is above all a sacrifice of communion (see page 122). For St. John, the blood that flows from the pierced side of Jesus is the source of life, especially in the sacramental action of the eucharist.

It is, above all, the author of the Epistle to the Hebrews who has developed a presentation of the redemption in ritual terms that he employs analogically. He is not thinking of the rites, properly so-called, of the eucharistic sacrifice. Speaking of the happening of the existential sacrifice of the cross completed by the eternal action of Jesus in heaven, he transposes the terms which belong to the Temple liturgy, and shows their analogical and transcendent realization. How the sacrifice of purification is carried out is known to the readers. But in the death and ascension of Jesus must be seen a Temple not made by man (heaven); a high priest who carries his own blood and passes through the veil of the sanctuary once and for all, so that he does not need to perform his sacrifice again and again, but he is always in a state of intercession, and the purification which he confers on man in God's name has a permanent validity.

We may note a fine point in the matter of translation. In Chapter 2, verse 17, several translations have: "it was right that he should in all things be made like unto his brethren . . . to expiate the sins of his people." The Greek term *hilaskesthai* does not take *sins* as its direct object. It means *to render* a person *propitious;* the accusative indicates what the action concerns. Therefore, the expiation here also signifies that Jesus intercedes for us so that God will show himself propitious. We are purified by God acting through his Mediator.

Therefore, a difference in perspective is to be noted between the language of the Bible and the language of the present day. In the former, *expiation* designates first of all a purification for which God provides man with the instrument, while in modern terms *expiation* signifies rather the deadly consequences of sin, or the punishment which the guilty impose on themselves.

This latter meaning is connected with *satisfaction,* which we will now examine.

3. *Satisfaction-Reparation*

The term *satisfaction* is not used in the Bible when speaking of the mystery of the redemption. It is introduced during the Patristic period when the Fathers were examining the relations between sin on the one hand, and the justice and mercy of God on the other.

The Middle Ages saw the spread of a theory which stated that sin causes the sinner to contract a debt which is "infinite", and that only Jesus Christ is able to pay this debt. St. Thomas does not admit that divine pardon, in order to be just, is necessarily conditioned by suffering a "satisfactory"—*i.e.,* adequate—penalty. The following is a very clear text: "When it is a question of a personal offense, the judge can then remit the entire punishment . . . God can, without injuring anyone, remit the offense of sin without exacting any penalty: *Si Deus voluisset absque omni satisfactione hominem a peccato liberare, contra justitiam non fecisset*" (*Summa,* III, q. 46, a. 2, ad 3).

Today Thomists insist that in the satisfaction which Christ made there is no question either of commutative justice or of vindicative justice. The mystery of the redemption is essentially a mystery of mercy, of the merciful and gratuitous charity of God. But where would mercy be, if the cross were a settling of accounts, in which neither of the parties wishes to "give" anything at all? Where would the "free gift" be, if the cross were to act as the balance between the penal exactions of God and a penalty being worked off by humanity? If it be answered that Christ, who pays the debt required by justice, is the gift of the Father's mercy, we have the whole problem back again: God would be exacting in justice to himself what he makes possible only by his mercy. What meaning can this have for a philosophy which opposes the exigencies of justice to the free gift of mercy?

In order to work out a valid understanding of the redemption-as-satisfaction, it would be better to put back into the real situation the action of God, and to distinguish in its interpretation *the different emphases that are due to different mentalities.*

(a) The Semitic mind thinks in terms of *interpersonal relations, the initiative for which comes from God.* The "justice" of God consists in bringing about the existence of good relations. Therefore, there is no difficulty in seeing it side by side with his "merciful love", which inclines toward man in order to "redeem" him.

When man sins, he excites the "anger" of God and his "jealousy": two terms that signify the reaction of God to the attitude in which man comes to oppose him, and by which (attitude) man wishes to establish with other (gods) relations that only have a meaning and a legitimacy with respect to Yahweh. God then takes the initiative of *corrective punishment,* so that he can later take the attitude and initiative of pardon. He wants to bring the sinner to conversion; as soon as man's refusal of God ceases, the cause of God's anger disappears; he has no need of man's gifts as appeasement. It is only in the case of obstinate refusal that the divine punishment becomes vindictive, that is, brings about the destruction of the evil by the perdition of its author.

What is the make-up of the sinner's response to the action of God which attempts to change his attitude? The man who finds in chastisement the light to remedy his willful blindness will "confess" to God that he repents of his sin; he will protest that he has not hardened his heart; he will confidently ask for forgiveness.

A double motive found in the heart of God is the basis of the trust of his repentant people: namely, concern for his glory and (above all) the fidelity of his merciful love. God himself takes care of his glory (Ps. 105, 8): he shows its splendor in the sight of his enemies, from whom the chosen people have been delivered that they may be converted. God also takes care of his merciful love. If we implore the forgiveness of our debts, it is because we have no right (by reason of any "payment") to the favor of God. This favor, that is, his pardon, is a pure gift of his mercy, and does not need to be invoked by any other motive. Therefore, it is God who gives his people the instrument of divine propitiation: he permits them to employ for this end the blood which is "sacred". And God continues by every means to bring his people back to him. *Reparation* for sin is shown particularly in the progress of the relation of friendship between God and man.

This viewpoint becomes precise in the New Testament. *Two parables,* each one complementary to the other, make us understand *what God exacts from the sinner.* In the parable of the Father whose younger son has left him, it is enough that sorrow be manifested for God to forgive him: there is not even any question of any other satisfaction than this witness to sorrow. In the parable of the insolvent debtor, if we read of debts it is to emphasize that man cannot pay them and that he has only to hope for salvation from God alone, who quite simply cancels all his indebtedness. All that is exacted is that he show himself merciful to others.

The "debt-theme", therefore, is not to be understood in the sense of "satisfaction" exacted by God for himself. If there is reparation to be made, it consists in witness to a fidelity once more assumed and accepted, manifesting itself in kindness to our neighbor.

As for the *role of Jesus,* nowhere is the statement made that it consists in paying a debt for us; above all, there is no mention of a debt which he pays to his Father. But, without being moved thereto by any personal punishment which he does not merit, and without confessing sorrow—since he has never turned away from God—it is out of love that he comes to share the sad condition which is the consequence of the sins of men. So Jesus brings about the disappearance of the motif of God's *anger,* as he reestablishes humanity in the response of justice. The merciful Father has sent him for this reason, and "in Christ (*i.e.,* present in his action) God reconciled the world to himself" (2 Cor. 5, 19).

(b) The mentality at the basis of individual *anthropocentrism,* which we find especially in the pagan thought of the ancient Greeks, some traces of which remain in a certain "Christian humanism" which is subjective in character, has two distinguishing features. Pagan anthropocentrism looks to the happiness of man, in particular to his interior perfection, and it sees the divinity according to the expanded ideal of man. To its way of thinking, sin destroys the harmonious unity of man; it precipitates him by an inner necessity into unhappiness; and it provokes the vengeance of the gods. Threatened in his happiness, man attempts to appease the divinity by gifts, or to regain the favor of the gods by the performance of difficult actions which contain a certain *merit.* But when he reflects on it, the man who is concerned for his own personality knows that *the reestablishment of the inner harmonious unity* depends in the last analysis on his own liberty. His agreement with others, even with impersonal Nature, and with God, will be the fruit of his interior balance.

Christians who have an affinity for this kind of anthropocentrism will try to encourage its extreme consequences. They will insist on humble and trusting prayer, which is as necessary for conversion as it is for the pardon received as a gesture of the divine mercy. And they will remember that the interior forces of man, his balance, and his happiness are themselves gifts of God. In the mediation of Christ, it will be particularly the aspect of merit due to a difficult action, and the invitation to interior mortification which will have their attention.

(c) The third mentality to be met with puts the accent on *the objective order, exacted by justice in a juridical sense*. The exactions of this justice are determined *a priori,* independent of a situation, and of anything which may be peculiar to the situation. God is the supreme guardian of order: this is his privilege. And, in the abstract, God himself is required to respect order and justice, as well as to reestablish them when they have been violated by creatures. Sin is a violation of order; in offending God, man also inflicts harm on the established order. The reestablishment of this order requires *a satisfaction which is the equivalent of the wrong done*. However, God never suffers harm, either in his person or in his possessions, which no man can snatch from him, but only in his "glory". It is, therefore, rather *a compensation of honor* that is required.

According to this terminology, it is said that Jesus, by his obedience, especially on the cross (see page 117f.), renders to his Father an honor greater than the dishonor caused by man's sin. But since a terminology focused on measurement (satisfaction, superabundant, more, less, etc.) is far from adequate in what concerns honor, and even more imperect in what concerns the glory of God, the term *satisfaction* will be replaced with great advantage by the term *reparation,* which is more in keeping with biblical terms.

The Council of Trent employs in the first place the biblical terms of *reconciliation,* (biblical) *justice, sanctification, redemption,* and it adds that "Christ has made satisfaction for us to God the Father" (Denz. 799). Note that there is here no blending of images, which are valid only in different contexts. Redemption is accomplished by the payment of a ransom, but it is not paid to anyone; Christ makes satisfaction to his Father, but this satisfaction-reparation is not made after the manner of a payment. Therefore, we must avoid the blockage which results in saying in the same breath that Christ makes satisfaction to his Father by paying him a ransom. To reach a unified view of the complementary aspects of the reality, we must proceed not by mixing terminologies, but by reflection which re-weighs the terms of the whole synthesis, and by the use of expressions that are suitable to that synthesis. We will attempt to do so in a legitimate manner by a consideration of the categories and formulations of contemporary thought.

(d) In regard to *the contemporary mind* we select two characteristics that are valuable for thinking about and expressing the truths of revelation as they concern the redemption: it is personalist, and it is concerned with man-in-his-situation. To put it another way, it emphasizes the constitutive *liberty* of the human person, and it sees this liberty essentially in relation to the *"given" features* of the existential situation of man. These relations are of four kinds:

(1) man is *in the world;* therefore, his liberty achieves its development in relation to the world;

(2) the person is *in the community;* therefore, liberty has an essential relation to charity;

(3) human life is situated *in an action of God;* therefore, good and evil are to be envisaged in relation to the active design of God;

(4) man is *in time,* that is, in a relation to the past and the future, and even to a future situation which will go beyond time.

This is not the place to give an elaborate exposition of the meaning to be attributed, according to these four categories, to God's call, man's sin, the function of the Mediator, and the role of the Church. We may note simply that *reparation* can be expressed in a way which respects the synthesis of the essential aspects.

The accent will be placed on the dimension of inter-personal relations with God: Jesus reestablishes man in *his response* to God, an obedient response which makes reparation for man's disobedience and his refusal to love God. But these inter-personal relation cannot subsist unless the liberty of all parties is ensured. Therefore, each man is called upon *to commit himself with all his liberty to participation in the existential way of Christ,* the Head of renewed humanity. In other words, the redemption is the reestablishment of a personal "inter-subjectivity". In this perspective, the liberty of one party is not seen as a compensation for the liberty of the other. But it will be recalled that human liberty can only be fully realized *in a communion of personal liberties.* Therefore, the redemption has an ecclesial character, that is, a character of union with Christ in a human community.

Thirdly, reparation has a dimension of "objectivity", too. It is not solely a matter of interior liberty and spiritual communion; it is also and essentially situated in the external world. Sin has its "objective" effects; they are expressed in the body; they are graven in our soul by its tendency to evil; they are manifest in society, which is the exterior aspect of community, and, by this fact, they exercise an influence on the liberty of others: sin is a "scandal".

This is why redemption is also carried out in terms of a reparation for the objective effects of sin. It will demand of the sinner the *mortification* of his sinful tendencies, and it will be shown in public by the *witness* of sorrow, regret, conversion and restored fidelity. Christ had no need either to repent, or to be converted, or to mortify himself; but he accomplished his function of redemption "in the world", especially by the "witness" of his fidelity to charity, the compensation and the reparation for the non-witness given in the public expression of sin (scandal) in the world.

This witness of Jesus was presented with its greatest reparative force on the cross (see page 117f.); but it attained all its force of proclamation only in the manifestation of the glorious and immortal communion of Christ with the Father. The witness of Christ calls for and makes possible our own, as participation in the redemption "in the world".

Finally, since the world is situated within time, it follows that there is a *temporal dimension* to the work of Jesus and to our own. This last is the foundation of the "temporal punishment" which still has a meaning, even after the perfection of the action of Jesus in his "hour", and even after the pardon received by the individual Christian in the sacraments.

4. *The Redemptive Worth of the Blood of Christ*

The blood of Christ is a physical reality, both when it is shed on the cross and when, in a different manner, it is given, united to the risen body, in the eucharist. But its redemptive value is to be found essentially in *its relationship with an action performed by Christ* (on the cross and in the eucharist). To render explicit the value of this action, we will make use of three terminologies whose validity we have just reviewed. We will attempt to make explicit the role of the blood, first in its biblical context of redemption (with the sacrifice of communion) and of purification, then in theological speculation on satisfaction-reparation.

In the biblical context, *blood* is *life* because it contains life. Life belongs to God. Blood comes from God, keeps the living being under the protection of God, and is destined to return to God. This return is expressed in worship. God approves the oblation of what is destined to return to him. God even institutes the blood-rite as a means of communion (at Sinai) and of reconciliation-purification (in the Temple). God forbids all sacrifice of human blood, thus emphasizing the respect due to life, because all human life is especially "sacred".

The *blood which is shed* has, therefore, two quite different meanings: (1) *the violent death* of a man is a profanation; this shedding of blood cries to heaven for vengeance; (2) blood shed in the course of ceremonies of worship does not derive its value from death, but from the fact of its meaning as *a return to God;* this is a value that stems from consecration. God accepts it as the expression of what belongs to him and he makes use of the blood, now sacred, as a means of sanctification, *i.e.,* purification, communion.

The *blood of Christ* is *lutron,* a means of redemption,

in two ways at one and the same time. It is the means of liberation and purification by which God saves his people and reconciles them to himself, in his Son become man.

God does not directly will the violent death of his Son, for that is a desecration. But:

(1) The Father expects that the Son will be faithful to *charity, even when this fidelity becomes extremely onerous because of the hostility of men.* This is "the cup" which Jesus must drink: fidelity even under conditions of extreme difficulty. He pays the *ransom (lutron,* first meaning) of perfect obedience, in charity, even to the cruel and ignominious death caused by the sinful enmity of men. This charity delivers us and will be communicated to us in the form of union with God.

(2) This death, accepted in this "spirit" (Heb. 9, 14) becomes for Christ himself the "return" to the Father (Jn. 13, 1). *This return by the way which the Father has ordained for him* constitutes his sacrifice. His blood becomes for us the means-of-propitiation (*lutron,* second meaning). By participating in the sacrifice of Christ we are purified and we enter into communion with God.

As for the earlier theological context of satisfaction, the function of blood has practically been reduced to that of *death-of-reparation.* The best theologians, even while recalling that death is for men a punishment of sin, have not considered Christ on the cross as being, in his own person, punished by God. They have emphasized that the acceptance of death, out of obedience and through love, constituted a reparation for sin which is the refusal to obey and to love. This acceptance is an act freely accomplished. In what sense? Christ has perfectly subjected his will to the will of the Father. For both, death was not either directly willed, *i.e.*, inflicted or sought, respectively; nor was it passively accepted as inevitable; it was indirectly willed, that is, accepted as the condition of a fidelity confronted by the persecution of the unfaithful. We have shown (p. 74) that the reparation lies above all in *the witness* which is opposed to the scandal.

The theology of the redemptive death needs to be completed by a theology of *the redemptive resurrection.* The theories that speak only of the death-satisfaction are not sufficiently in line with the whole of the primitive tradition, which, without neglecting the function of the cross, emphasized the salvific function of the resurrection. The blood is the gift of life. Christ not only shed his blood in death, but, risen from the dead, he also gives it in *the sacrament of life.* He not only surrendered his earthly life for us, he also communicates to us his risen life. The gift which Christ gives us, he gives in the name of his Father, in the power of the Holy Spirit. But, it is first of all *to* his Father that Christ gives himself. From this point of view, what is the function of the blood?

In what sense does Christ offer his blood to his Father, and in what sense does the Father accept the blood of his Son?

According to the biblical theme of redemption implying a ransom, it is God who redeems his people. He does so by acting through his Messiah. He pays the ransom for this redemption, but he does not pay it *to* anyone. Still less is it God *from whom* man must be redeemed. The blood of Christ is not demanded as ransom by the Father; it is neither offered nor accepted in this sense. Christ, who redeems us in the name of the Father, purchases us once more *for* the Father (Acts 20, 28). On the other hand, by freely dying on the cross in order to redeem us (not paying a ransom to anyone) *Christ existentially "offers" to his Father his fidelity, which is signified in this supreme testimony.* And the Father "accepts" this sign for what it signifies: the fidelity of his Son. "He that loses his life will save it." "I lay down my life, that I may take it again" (in Greek, *hina:* the end) (Jn. 10, 17). Jesus gives his life in order that he may find it again in a better form. The Father who accepts his fidelity, witnessed even unto death, raises up Jesus from the dead.

This existential offering is a free action manifested in an event: the return to the Father, becoming eternal in a continual encounter, realizing a mutual giving. But this reality can be expressed in *terms taken from ritual offering.* It is then possible to say that Christ, in his passage from earth to heaven, accomplished a "sacrifice" of communion, more perfect than all the ritual sacrifices of the Old Testament. This ritual vocabulary, employed by assimilation, is found again in the theme of purification-expiation.

In the two ritual sacrifices (of communion, as on Mt. Sinai, and of purification, as in the Temple, both reunited in a single existential sacrifice in the case of Christ) *the blood is the sign of divine intervention.* Because it is sacred, the blood employed in the rite is the efficacious sign of communion and of purification, or, in other words, of consecration and of re-consecration after the desecration caused by sin. Therefore, in this case, it is God who gives the blood for the sacrifice: that is, he permits it to be employed ritually, and he attaches an efficacy to it. Thus, he has permitted Christ to accept the shedding of his blood in a sacrifice of communion and of purification for us.

This blood is offered to God, not as if it were a creature which was not already consecrated to him (the
blood is sacred), but in the sense that the priest is carrying out *a symbolical action* expressive of the fact that
the blood is returning to God to whom it belongs.
Christ, in giving his life back to God in an act of
obedience and love, offers his blood in *an existential
act of return to God,* an existential act that can be expressed also in ritual terms employed analogically. The
Father accepts this blood, not as a thing which has not
been consecrated and now is so, but the Father approves
the gesture expressive of the return of the blood (an
existential act assimilated to a ritual gesture). God accepts the gesture of the blood given *in circumstances
that make of the gesture a witness to the fidelity of the
one acting.*

All of this is true of the cross united to the resurrection, that is, of the gift which Christ made definitively
on the cross and in which he now lives in heaven. When
we use the terms of the offering of the blood in speaking
of *the eucharist* (see page 86), important shades of
meaning are added. Here one uses a *ritual expression,*
no longer assimilated, but *formal;* except that the ritual
sacrifice of the eucharist is not an absolute sacrifice, but
a relative one, perfectly real, but made *in reference* to
the sacrifice of the cross and the state of oblation of
Christ in heaven. Here the rite does not directly signify
the gift, but *"the presence of the gift, rendered visible in
a symbol, in view of our participation."*

In the mass, Christ offers himself, that is, he renders
present in a sign, the gift realized on the cross and in
heaven. We offer Christ, that is, the priest manifests
efficaciously that Christ who is present is offering himself in the name of all men; and the faithful, by associat-

ing themselves with the rite carried out by the priest, associate themselves by a personal commitment with the sacrifice of Christ. The Father accepts this oblation, that is, he receives with favor the existential gift that Christ is making, and the gift of ourselves that we are making in union with Christ. Accepting this gift, the Father makes it become more and more perfect in communion. Communion consists in our participation within the Church in the communion in which Christ lives with his Father, a communion that is already glorious for Christ, a "pilgrim" communion, *in via,* where we are concerned; in both cases, it is the gift of the Holy Spirit.

At the very heart of the eucharistic celebration, this whole manifestation of the presence of Christ in his sacrifice and our participation with him is expressed ritually by the institutional recital, including the "Do this . . ." and by the sacramental communion. It is important to insist on this in catechesis. As for the other prayers in which frequently occur the terms "we offer the body and the blood of Jesus Christ", care must be taken to interpret them as so many *means of making explicit the prayer in which the whole rite is saturated,* and not as so many successive and distinct moments of the offering. In particular, the offertory cannot be explained separately from the consecration: its whole meaning consists in being an explicit preparation for it.

The importance of the eucharist resides in its relationship to the continuation of Christ's redemptive work and in our participation in it.

5. *The Meaning of the Term "for Us" in the Redemptive Work of Christ*

Redemption is accomplished by Jesus Christ for us, and by us in union with Jesus Christ.

The Latin texts (whether of the translation of the Bible or of the teaching Church) frequently state that Christ suffered, or that he died *"pro nobis"*, for us. It is possible to distinguish several senses of the Latin *pro* and the English *for*. We should recall that these terms applied to the action of Jesus Christ were first applied to it in the Greek of the New Testament. And we may consider, apropos of each meaning, what interpretation is proper concerning the active part we should assume in the mystery of the redemption. This part will consist first of all in an active "reception", but it comprises, too, a conformity of action.

(1) The Greek *hyper* is the term used in the great majority of cases where the redemption is being considered (Jn. 17, 19; Gal. 2, 20; Rom. 5, 8; 8, 32; Gal. 2, 20; 1 Pet. 3, 18); it can signify two aspects of the word *for*:

(a) an *orientation: in our favor*. By his action Christ wins for us signal advantages; the term does not say expicitly that we have anything else to do except to receive them.

(b) a *representation* (one person representing a group): *in our name*. This term indicates much more completely the relation existing between Christ's action and ours. Jesus acts *in our name, as our leader, as our Head, in union with us*. These meanings correspond to the totality of the mystery of salvation revealed even in the Old Testament: there is always a question of the union of a given individual, having a function with reference to the group, and of the group "represented" in its head. This union can be termed "solidarity". However, in personalist thought today, solidarity does not safeguard the distinction of persons; rather, they are lost sight of in the perspective of "all for all". If we wish

to give greater emphasis to the personal distinction existing between Christ and each individual man, and at the
same time emphasize the ontological unity binding them
together, it seems preferable to say *in communion with,*
or *in participation with.*

This interpretation highlights the role of active collaboration which Christ expects of each of the members
of his mystical body.

(2) The Greek *anti,* much more rarely used in the
context of the redemption (Mt. 20, 28; cf. Is. 53, 11-12),
may be translated in three possible ways:

(a) With the meaning of *a substitution: in our
stead.*

The idea of substitution hardly tallies with the two
principal aspects of sin, and therefore, not with the
concept of redemption either: the aspect of personal
liberty, and the aspect of inter-personal relations, especially when we remember that it is God who takes the
initiative in the latter. Therefore, the Bible, in its personalist concern, nowhere affirms that there is a substitution, whether in guilt, in punishment, or in the burden
or ransom independent of sin.

When it states that "God carries our burdens", it does
not have him carry them in our stead. When it says
of the servant, or of Christ: "He carries (and takes
away) our sins", it in no sense affirms that God considers an innocent man guilty instead of the sinners,
nor that he punishes him in their place, nor that he
"displaces" the punishment, removing it from the guilty
to the innocent.

These phrases signify that God intervenes in the
onerous conditions of redemption and that the Suffering
Servant, like Christ, participates in this onerous condition of the human situation caused by sin. Moreover,

and this is even true of the aspect of reparation exterior to the person, substitution does away with our function: the man who finds a substitute to pay his debt, does not need to pay the creditor himself. It would be false to assume that we are "even" with God.

(b) With the meaning of *a compensation given* by Christ. Again, this can be understood in two ways: either *"as a counterweight to our sins"*, or *"as supplying for our* (relative) *powerlessness to make reparation for our sins"*.

According to St. Thomas, Christ's satisfaction places within humanity, to the honor of God, a good superior to the evil brought there by sin.[2] But if we hold exclusively to this meaning of the term, we run the risk of accepting the faulty interpretation of substitution. On the contrary, by taking the two of them together, we return to the valid interpretation of representation.

Whatever may be the fact of the relative ability a man has to make reparation for his own sins, the most radical powerlessness of each man taken individually lies in the fact that he does not represent the whole human race. This is precisely the role of Christ. Thus, St. Thomas says: "Given that man was not capable of satisfying for the sin of the whole human race, God gave him as the author of satisfaction (*satisfactorem*) his Son".[3] To the emphasis put on the totality of the sin, should correspond the emphasis put on the free participation that characterizes our relationship with Christ. The term *"vicarious satisfaction"* does not occur in the writings of St. Thomas. When one uses it, one means

[2] Cf. *Summa Theol.*, III, q. 48, a. 2; q. 49, a. 4.
[3] Cf. *Summa Theol.*, III, q. 46, a. 1, ad 3.

the satisfaction accomplished "for" us. The term can, therefore, be understood as meaning *representation,* but unfortunately it is too often taken to mean *substitution,* and this must be avoided.

Finally, the Greek *anti* can be translated a third way:

(c) with the sense of a *counterpart received* by Christ: *in exchange for us.* As the image of a difficult bargain implies that of a ransom paid to someone, the result obtained from this ransom is some possession received in exchange. This is what is said of the Servant of Yahweh: he receives the nations in exchange for his life. In the same way, Christ acquires us in exchange for his own fidelity in difficult circumstances, and he gives us back to the Father for whom he has purchased us. In this sense, the term *anti* has the same meaning as the term *hyper:* a costly fidelity receives in exchange the liberation of those in favor of whom it has been maintained.

We may note, parenthetically, that when it is said that Christ suffers *for our sins,* this is a translation of the Greek *dia* or *eis,* and it means that Christ suffers "because of our sins" or "with a view to the remission of our sins", and for us, who are sinners, in the different meanings of this expression.

6. *The Eucharistic Participation in the Paschal Way of Christ the Redeemer*

The bond between the eucharist and the redemption is seen as it should be when we place ourselves, first of all, in a biblical perspective, and then support our thinking with the theology of the mystical body and the declarations in the Constitution on the Liturgy promulgated by Vatican II.

(a) *Biblical Sources*

As we have already shown, the Old Testament places the redemption in a double perspective. We will note here that each one has a corresponding and particular mode in the liturgy, and we will show how the two existential perspectives and the two liturgical modes are united in the eucharist instituted by Jesus Christ.

Given the material which the reader already has before him, a few brief indications are all that are needed here.[4]

The basic historic event of the Old Testament with its three elements—the Exodus, the sojourn in the desert, and the entrance into the Promised Land—has a trans-historic or a supra-historic significance for the redemption: the people of God leave the land of slavery, in the desert they go through a period of trial, and they enter into the land of God's blessings. In the center of this *existential journey* is placed the covenant; it is concluded in a blood-rite which is *a communion sacrifice*. At the "hour" of this divine intervention *a memorial* is instituted (its meaning is enriched in the course of centuries) in order to render possible for every generation of the people the liturgical participation in the redemption and in the covenant.

Development of the spiritual experience gives rise to an *interiorization*. The people need a *redemption from sin* and a return to the unity of God's friendship. It must take the form of a *spiritual journey* which consists in detachment from sin, remaining faithful to God and in once again finding union with God. The liturgical realization of this progress, which supposes its existential

[4] Cf. M. van Caster, "Eucharistic Catechesis Based on the Last Supper" in *Lumen Vitae* X (1955), pp. 328–98.

sincerity, is effected in another ritual sign of blood, which is a *sacrifice of purification*.

The central historical event of the New Testament, comprising the same three elements as the redemption of Israel, but in a much richer sense, realizes this trans-historical or supra-historical significance in the Head of the new people of God: Jesus leaves the land where sin exercises its oppressive force; he undergoes in perfect fidelity (charity, obedience) the supreme trial of death; and he enters with his risen humanity into full communion with God. The event of the "hour" of the New Testament, namely *the cross and resurrection* of Christ the redeemer, consists, therefore, in *the journey* in which Jesus shows himself *faithful to God in his existential way*.

Jesus has traveled this road as the leader of a line of march, at the head of the human race which God saves; in our name he is faithful to the end. This way is existentially our way. The institution of *the memorial* of Jesus-in-his-Hour is destined to render possible our participation in the action Christ the redeemer performs by being faithful to his paschal way. Jesus has chosen the circumstances and the expressions for this institution in such a way that the eucharistic liturgy clearly appears, in what is essential to it, as the transformation of the Jewish liturgy.

The moment is the Feast of the Passover; the material sign, which is never to be separated from the verbal sign, indicates that the "Hour", the happening, of the New Covenant, is coming to pass; it is concluded in the sign of blood, but the blood of Jesus is the blood shed for the remission of sins, that is, it is shed in a sacrifice of communion (as on Sinai) which is at the same time a sacrifice of purification (as in the liturgy of *Yom*

Kippur). The universal bread, which replaces the lamb of the Israelites, is the living Christ, now given to the new people of God. In the sacramental action, participation in the rite of the consecration and communion brings about the participation in the supernatural reality, which is the communion of Christians in Christ in his existential paschal way, by means of which is realized the covenant of love.

(b) *Theological Reflections on the Eucharistic Celebration*

The development of the theology of *the mystical body* has favored a better understanding of the unity, which exists and must be realized with ever greater perfection, between Christ and the Church, that is, not the hierarchy alone but the community of Christians within the Church.

The emphasis is now moving from the quasi-juridical aspect of the Church to the real aspect, as much in its ontological foundation as in its personalist realization. Thus, we are avoiding the abuses of the "substitution theory" by which the role of the person is suppressed because another takes his place; we are avoiding faulty perspectives in our theology of the sacrifice of the cross as also in our theology of the sacrifice of the mass. On the other hand, we are emphasizing the fact that *the role of Christ and the role of the members* (of the mystical body) *are essentially complementary,* and the second is as real as the first. Along the same line, we now recognize better *the communal character* of the liturgy, the official worship of the Mystical Body, and its personalist aspect requiring *a conscious and active participation* from each one.

This full and "real" conception also has its influence on *a renewed theology of the sacraments* and of the entire liturgy. Christ is acting in the Church, not simply in a juridical efficacy, in virtue of the institution of powers handed down through two millennia, but according to an efficacious ontological presence communicating itself. Thus, the sacramental signs should not be reduced to minimal conditions of juridical validity, but they must normally be recognized as *mediation of personalist encounter*. This is particularly true of *the eucharist*. In it the living and glorious Christ is active; and the mode of his action is "signified" to us by the sacramental signs he has instituted for this purpose. And these eucharistic signs require the action of the priest and of the faithful, each according to his role in the mystical body.

We will now explain how the meaning of the sacrifice of the mass corresponds to its liturgical form.

The meaning of the mass is that it renders the sacrifice of Christ present in such a way that Christians can participate in it. The *sacrifice of Christ,* namely, the oblation of himself which he made by dying on the cross and which he continues to offer in his glorious communion with the Father. This sacrifice, always *actual* and *present* in heaven, is the sacrifice of the cross in its glorious term. It is rendered present (on earth) by a rite that signifies its presence. It is not at all necessary that the eucharistic rite be a "figurative" sign of the death on the cross; by the very nature of its meaning, it is required, and it is enough that this sign be "indicative" of the presence which it effects and can effect because Christ instituted it for that purpose. The sign is clear: it is the words which "signify" that Christ is making himself present in a sacrificial context.

The same is true for the second aspect, (inseparable from the first), the meaning of the mass as *participation*

by the Christians in the sacrifice of Christ: the sign is
the bread and wine, over which the words of consecration are pronounced that they may be taken in communion, and which Christians receive liturgically as
nourishment. The special efficacy on the plane of charity
among Christians is signified by the communal sharing
in the sacrificial meal. The active eucharistic signs are,
therefore, perfectly adapted to the meaning of the mass,
which is to render the sacrifice of Christ present in such a
way that we can take part in it. Our participation must,
therefore, on its side, seek to accord as perfectly as
possible with the sacrifice of Christ in the whole context
of the mystery of the redemption.

Remarkable testimony to the fact that it is really
according to these views that the Church is today making
her pronouncements and wishes to act, may be found in
several statements of the Constitution on the Liturgy
promulgated by Vatican Council II. The "movement" of
the return to the sources of our thinking in a context
which is fully realistic and communal is all the more
evident when we compare these statements with others
previously in common use.

From the first page of the "Introduction", the Fathers
of the Council have taken as a fundamental principle
the fact that in the liturgy "the work of our redemption
is being done", that is, continues its activity. (Art. 2)

In Chapter I this reality is explained. First, the event
(Art. 5): "In redeeming mankind and giving perfect
glory to God, he (Christ) achieved his task principally
by the paschal mystery of his blessed passion, resurrection from the dead, and glorious ascension." The more
common expressions often used to make the connection
between the redemption and the cross, without speaking
of the resurrection, and above all without explaining

that in the death-and-resurrection we are talking about a unique paschal mystery, whose elements cannot be separated from one another.

Then, attached to the event with its trans-historical significance, the liturgical celebration (Art. 6): we must see it in the total action of the Church. In the first place, to "proclaim that the Son of God, by his death and resurrection, has freed us from the power of Satan", that is the function of the preaching of the apostles and the task of the faith to be fulfilled by the faithful. In the second place, to "accomplish the work of salvation . . . by means of sacrifice and sacraments", namely, the function of conferring them and the task of participating in them. "By baptism men are plunged into the paschal mystery of Christ"—this is the initial sacramental celebration. "From that time onwards the Church has never failed to come together to celebrate the paschal mystery: reading those things 'which were in all the scriptures concerning him', celebrating the eucharist in which 'the victory and triumph of his death are again made present', and at the same time giving thanks 'to God for his unspeakable gift' in Christ Jesus, 'in praise of his glory', through the power of the Holy Spirit."

We have cited the text in an abbreviated form, but the Constitution expressly employs the term *repraesentaretur* and gives it for subject *mortis ejus victoria et triumphus.* The Council of Trent gives as subject for the same word *sacrificium in cruce peragendum,* and it is well known what controversies in interpretation this has given rise to. We must rejoice at this official re-interpretation. We can understand the term in the sense of 'making present', knowing that its subject is the reality, made eternal, of the glorious life triumphing over death.

In a word, it is the unique paschal mystery which is being celebrated; it is this mystery which is rendered liturgically present; it is the actually living Christ who is actually present in his continued sacrificial action; this activity is the same by which, on the cross, he committed his soul into the hands of his Father.

This sense of presence, actual and active, is confirmed and explained in the ramifications of the following paragraph (Art. 7): "Christ is always present to his Church, especially in her liturgical celebrations. He is present in the sacrifice of the mass, not only in the person of his minister . . . but especially under the eucharistic species. By his power he is present in the sacraments . . . He is present in his word, since it is he himself who speaks when the holy Scriptures are read in the Church . . . He is present, lastly, when the Church prays and sings."

Finally, we may note a few other precious indications given in "Chapter II". The text of Art. 47 returns in large part to the text of the Council of Trent; it recalls, namely, the institution of its reference to the sacrifice of the cross; at the same time—and this is worthy of note— it does not use again the term *repraesentaretur* and it does not accept a term meaning "to renew": expressions like these, which have serious reasons against them, were already quite widely used, although outside official texts; it chooses the term *perpetuaret*. "To perpetuate the sacrifice of the cross throughout the centuries"; this is done by continuing the sacrifice in the mode suitable to the later situation. This mode is indicated by the re-interpretation—also quite remarkable—contained in the following section of the text: "to entrust to his beloved spouse, the Church, a memorial of his death and resurrection". Once again the mention of the

resurrection has been added. And the eucharistic celebration is described farther on in several ways, among
which we draw attention to the term "paschal meal".
The Constitution cites the familiar antiphon *O sacrum
convivium, in quo Christus sumitur,* but it has replaced
in a significant manner the term "sacred meal" by the
term "paschal meal".

So clearly indicated an intention must bring us to
consider the eucharist at all times, whether explicitly or
implicitly, in its context of paschal redemption.

A summary formulation might be couched in the
following terms: the eucharist is the ecclesial liturgy of
the redeeming sacrifice, celebrated in communion by
Christ and his members. The priest has the function
of the minister, on the one hand with regard to Christ,
on the other with regard to the faithful. But the action
on which the entire celebration rests is the action of
Christ himself who is present; and all the faithful have
an active part to play in carrying out the prayers and
rites as well as in the "spiritual" sacrifice which is the
redemption itself.

Another point: the terminology of *merit* also requires,
in its turn, to be re-thought in a personalist way. It requires prudence in use and interpretation analogous to
that needed with regard to the "ransom paid". "Christ
merits our salvation; he merits for us; we merit with
him". None of these expressions should be interpreted
along hard juridical lines, as if merit corresponded to
a ransom paid to God, on whom it had acquired a certain claim. Merit, in the personalist sense, is the force
of ulterior union, which resides in an act of love that does
not yet result in perfect communion. The force of the
gift of self is accompanied by an availability-to-the-

other, and together they constitute an appeal for what cannot be forced, namely, the free gift of self by which the other will realize, or make actual on his side, communion.

By these acts of love performed on earth, and especially by his charity shown on the cross, Christ merits his own glorious communion with the Father. Since he acts as Head of the human race, he merits the communication of this love, which fills him as Head, to his members. The members, by personal commitment in acts vivified by this same charity, merit progress in the more perfect realization of communion.

7. *Our Fidelity Witnessed in the Trials of the Apostolate.*

In this way, above all, we participate in the existential condition of Christ the redeemer and in his redemptive action.

The example of the saints, and especially of St. Paul, highlights what each of us experiences to a lesser degree, namely, that the life of the apostle is a tissue of joys and sorrows mutually influencing each other.

The apostle knows the joy of laboring at the most splendid task in the world, and sometimes of seeing surprising results. But he must impose upon himself the privation of many joys that would deflect his strength and consume his time. He will sometimes have to suffer the inopportune; he will always have to suffer fatigue. He will suffer from lack of success due to his own faults or his sins. On the other hand, the painful experience of our own sins can be put to the service of the apostolate, because it allows us to know from our own lives the situation of the sinner.

The peculiar and profound suffering of the Christian

who is struggling against the sin of the world, lies in this concern for sinners. It is mingled with profound joy because this concern is an eminent form of charity, of the kind which Christ showed to men. The union of priests and laymen in the apostolate here finds one of its most important realizations: all must imitate Christ in his manner of accomplishing the redemption; all are called to enter into participation with the situation of sinners, with a view to their conversion and sanctification. When the sinner, recognizing his fault, is ready for conversion, the apostle who is helping him, nonetheless suffers with him the horror stemming from the presence of the sin which they are combating together. But the case becomes even worse when those very people to whom the apostle wishes to show this love, turn against him; sometimes this is simply ill-humor, sometimes it will take the form of violent persecution; most often it is an opposition kept within narrower limits, but constitutes a heavy weight on the body and heart of the apostle.

The charity proper to the work of the redemption will manifest itself in the apostle by his accessibility and his perseverance in carrying the burden of the sins of others, like Christ, and with the strength that he draws from Christ. But if the apostle has the painful experience of the weight of all he has to bear, he is himself carried by the strength that he draws from Jesus Christ and by the joy that he finds in his confidence in God. Through consolation and desolation the apostle follows Jesus along the road of the work of redemption.

Our participation in the work of Christ the redeemer is never an imitation pure and simple. For Jesus was without sin, while we are still sinners, so that we have to be saved by him, and in the work that we are doing with

Christ to save others, there is always some influence of our own disordered tendencies. Although mixed with elements that must themselves be purified, our participation in the continuation of the redemption is real. *Essentially and freely we are following Christ the redeemer along the road to the building up of the kingdom of God and the salvation of men, the road which is also the road to the cross and the resurrection.*

8. *Religious Redemption and Temporal Liberation*

Therefore, this change in human existence effected by the salvation in which Jesus Christ makes us sharers, in what does it consist, and how is it brought about? In our answer to this question, we will have to recall the relation between the religious plane and the other levels of existence.

The supernatural action of God on man and on the world comes to us: (a) *from* the interior *to* the exterior; (b) *from* the exterior *to* the interior, for the transformation of the whole.

(a) *Beginning Within*

The transformation that grace brings takes place directly on the theological plane, that is, in the area of the relations of men to God. Therefore, grace directly reaches our interior life, the soul, and acts upon our liberty. The free action of man, vivified by grace, radiates on the whole of man, body and soul, and on all that man touches. But here we must distinguish different planes of existence:

The four principal levels of human life are: (1) *civilization,* or the mastery of techniques; (2) *culture,* or the development of particular human values; (3) *morality,* or the order of particular values in the totality of the person and of the human community; (4) *religion,* or man's relation to God.

Between these distinct levels there exists, at the same time, a requirement of unity, an ambiguity of meaning, and a distance of development.

All corporal and spiritual service, seen as an outward expression of charity, finds its place along this line.

Therefore, divine grace, acting on human liberty, will, if we collaborate with God, bring about transformations on each of these levels, but only as a result of long patience and at the price of inevitable, if temporary, loss of balance.

Moreover, the Christian spirituality of *incarnation, i.e.,* of grace in all that is human, always remains dependent on a spirituality of *conversion,* because what is human is still continually affected by the consequences of sin. Finally, this spirituality must always be sufficiently eschatological, or oriented toward a surpassing of the terrestrial and temporal situation.

(b) *Beginning Outside*

The distinction we must keep in mind here is the distinction between *the temporal situation* and the *eschatological situation.* To bring about total and definitive salvation, God will act miraculously by a supernatural action that will bring about the resurrection of the body and the new world suitable to the condition of fully saved mankind. In the meantime, more sporadic miracles and a certain corporal action of the sacraments give us premonitory signs of this accomplishment. But during the temporal period, God habitually acts only by the exterior action of the "signs" he gives us of his deeds, notably in his Word, manifested in all the forms of *testimony* to his salvific action, and his *sacraments* in which he gives us his grace in a special manner.

The *profane* or *secular structure* of the world is not, therefore, changed. But because of the presence of Christ in the world, a presence continued by his Church, there is in the world something more than the world natural to man; and there is in the world a "call" to consider it in a perspective that is more vast, namely, to consider it in the perspective of the eschatological design of God.

In the exterior world around him, the Christian comes to recognize two aspects of transformation in connection with grace. On the one hand, the Christian no longer sees simply a world detached from God, but a world in which *he recognizes the signs of the Christian revelation* and of re-action to grace. On the other, he sees in the world a call to his own action, *to make his own witness* to the action of God and the presence of Christ in his Church *shine with ever greater brilliance*.

The synthesis of interiority and exteriority, each influenced by the action of "salvation", takes place in the acceptance of the call to charity, and in the living witness to that charity which the Holy Spirit communicates to us.

CHAPTER III

SYNTHESIS AND CONCLUSIONS FOR CATECHESIS

The data of the genetic presentation permit of a valid *integration* of the constitutive elements of revelation. Our analysis has comprised a *dis-integration* of certain false obstacles which have given rise to deviant interpretations, and the *re-integration* of the essential elements expressed in personalist terms. The catechetical conclusions will have to do with the mentality of the catechist, the choice of terms, and the structure of a valid schema leading toward a synthesis.

1. *The Religious Mentality of the Catechist*

The most direct catechetical question is often couched in the following terms: "How can we present . . . (in this case, the redemption)?" Now it is clear that the answer presupposes a "mentality" which is itself sometimes questionable. Should not the question be: "How does the catechist represent to himself what he wants to present to others?" This question is a capital one, for a sort of osmosis goes on between the mentality of the catechist and the tone which the faith of those catechized will assume. Behind one or another expression, its choice, its accent and its interpretation, there is a basic mentality being transmitted, a way of considering the matter of revelation.

Between revelation in its primitive form and the presentation that corresponds to the mentality of the catechist a deviation has sometimes slipped in. This deviation may, on the one hand, take the form of a *foreshortening* of the field of vision, or, on the other, of a *surplus* of additional points of teaching which are nothing more than so many disputed points, the fruit of human reasoning. This will be disastrous in the case of words taken out of their context, instead of realities understood in all their authentic meaning, which are allowed to structure the course.

One begins by isolating a word, for example, in the catechism (where it appears as a translation . . . of a translation); then one elaborates the current, or dictionary, meaning of the word to show what it means; then one comes to the conclusion that faith contains such and such a statement, which, in fact, is quite foreign to it, at least in the sense that one is advancing. On the contrary: each text must be put back into its context. Then divine revelation, which is existential at its point of origin as in its actuality, and which contains a vast wealth of shades of meaning, will not be reduced to some kind of a pat summary. And a summary dating from one or another epoch in the evolution of thought, will not be put forward in an absolute manner without reference to its sources. It will then be possible to borrow a terminology in keeping with what is valid in contemporary thought and to recapture the authentic meaning of revelation in its sources.

We may apply this to the terminology of the redemption, situated, as we have just situated it, in a context that is Semitic and contemporary as well as clearly personalist.

2. *Terminology Based on Valid Emphases*

(a) In keeping with biblical texts and with modern personalist thought, it is proper to insist upon:

—God's initiative; his attitude toward man is always favorable; this is as true in the redemption as in the creation;

—the reality of the collaboration of each man in all that he is able to do himself;

—the unity between (1) the interiorization, or liberty, of sin and reparation, and (2) their exteriorization-in-the-world;

—the three aspects of the redemptive role of "mediators"; each of these aspects is to be found also in Christ in a transcendant form; each aspect is continued in the threefold collaboration of the Church in the work of redemption;

—the internal connection that unites the preaching of Jesus and his death on the cross; it is the foundation of the meaning of the "fidelity" of which the cross is the ultimate witness;

—the internal connection that unites the cross and the resurrection: these are two "moments" of a unique dialogue still going on;

—the double aspect of the redemption: (1) in a restricted sense it is simply the removal of evil; (2) in its fullest sense, it has also the aspect of the restoration of goodness;

—the double aspect, negative and positive, of the "gift";

—*the indefectible bond between the Father and the incarnate Son;*

—*the participation of Head and members,* each according to his function, and the impossibility of anyone assuming the function of another or substituting for him;

—the importance of our progressive conversion and of our witnessing to the redemption as coworker;

—the distance on this earth and the eschatological unity—already present *in germ*—which exist between (1) religious redemption, and (2) temporal liberation;

—the central reality of charity, and the essential "way" which is the paschal "journey" (see page 106f.).

(b) *Our choice* of expressions will be determined in accord with these valid emphases.

1. *The Father and the Son*

God the Father redeems us by his Son; the Father reconciles us to himself in his Son. The Father gives us his Son in order to deliver us. The Son manifests the power and the mercy of the Father who saves us. The Father gives the Son the power to deliver us and the charity necessary to pay the price for our deliverance. According to the merciful will of the Father, Jesus drank the cup of bitterness prepared by sinners.

2. *Jesus and Man*

Jesus responds to the Father in our name as the Head of the body of which we are the members. He placed himself in a position to share our lot. He reestablished the true response which had been lacking. Jesus fulfills his role as Head; we must carry out our role as members.

3. *The Cross*

Without undergoing punishment himself, Jesus has share our (existential) situation even to the death we undergo as punishment for our sins. The witness of love, which Jesus gave to his Father's honor in his death, makes up for and surpasses the injury done to God's glory by the sins of men. Jesus offers himself to the Father; he offers him his obedience and his love in his fidelity. He gives his life, his blood, by accepting death in circumstances that make of it a testimony of fidelity. Jesus offers himself as the perfect sacrifice, for he returns to the Father by the way the Father has chosen; he enters into a glorious communion with his Father, and he becomes the living instrument of our purification.

4. *The Resurrection*

The risen Jesus realizes salvation fully in his own person, for he receives its immortal plenitude. Christ lives in an eternal response to the gift of the Father. The Risen Jesus saves us in a positive manner by communicating a new life to us; this new life is a participation in his charity and the seed of our own resurrection. Seated at the right hand of the Father, Christ sends us the Holy Spirit.

5. *The Eucharist in the Redemption*

In the eucharist the work of the Redemption is being done; that is, it is there *in act,* because it is there that Jesus expresses himself in the gift of himself and that we associate ourselves to his love. In the mass we celebrate, by participating in it, the sacrifice of Jesus. We offer Christ and we offer ourselves. We share in the sacrifice of his body and his blood in the same sense Jesus gave to the sacrifice, namely, as an act of returning to the Father and as a witness of fidelity in reparation for sin. The sacrifice of the mass is the efficacious rite that makes visible the sacrifice of Jesus, begun on the cross and continued in heaven, an efficacious rite that makes us participants in the sacrificial act of Jesus. The mass renews, day by day, the rite which makes present the sacrifice realized on the cross and in heaven, and which makes Christians the sharers in this one sacrifice.

The priest acts in the name of Jesus Christ; the priest who carries out the rite is the minister of Christ who is offering the sacrifice. The priest represents Jesus in the exercise of this function. Christ fulfills his sacerdotal function by the ministry of the visible priest. Our participation must be an actively sincere one; our ritually expressed commitment must have a vital expression in all our actions. The eucharist is the ecclesial liturgy of the redeeming paschal sacrifice, celebrated in communion by Christ and his members.

3. *To Establish a Schema Leading to a Synthesis*

It is not enough to give a summary of the essential facts. It is also necessary to unite in the interpretation of the facts the three essential dimensions of the work of redemption.

(1) Therefore, *objectivity* cannot be so stressed that the presentation becomes overly materialized (in "things"). For example, God creates man and imposes on him (over and above?) a prohibition. Man violates this prohibition and thus commits sin. Sin is an obstacle between God and man, a debt (*i.e.,* a sum of money that must be paid: *a thing*). Man is incapable of paying it. Christ pays it instead of man by dying on the cross. Now we are freed from our sins by the merits of Christ which are applied to us (a "materialized" operation).

But suppose God were to remit our debt without exacting payment, requiring simply the goodwill manifested by our compassion toward our neighbor, as Jesus said (Mt. 18, 25)? On the other hand, if Jesus has paid the debt and has died instead of us, why do we still have to pay and to undergo death?

(2) Nor can the presentation be exclusively *subjective*. For example: God gave man freedom so that man would use it in its fundamental sense of a life willed by God. But man acted freely according to the sense which he himself gave to his life, setting himself up as the judge of good and evil. Sin consists in the abuse of freedom; in order to do away with sin, it is necessary and sufficient that man freely repudiates his self-sufficiency and returns (be converted) to God so as to act according to his divine will.

No man can act for me; where sin is concerned the freedom of one man cannot be substituted for the freedom of another. Christ's actions are only powerful examples that rouse my freedom to conversion of self. But what are the consequences of the fact that my liberty is "incarnated" in the world, in what concerns sin as well as in what concerns conversion? Again, where will the freedom that has become sinful find the strength, unaided, to return to God?

(3) A *valid* synthesis requires us to put the emphasis on the inter-personal relations, that is, on *"inter-subjectivity"*; it supposes that we will take into account liberty (subjectivity) and the incarnation of human liberty in the world (objectivity).

By giving life to man-in-the-world as partner in a dialogue, God calls him to live in relations of dependence and love with himself. In the normal trial of his liberty, man refuses to do so. Thus he brings into the world the fact and the scandal of sin: this is the objectification of his sinful will. And the consequences are especially manifest in the "painful death" he has to undergo. But humanity is destined to find the accomplishment of its unity in its relationship with the Son of God made Man.

Jesus does not permit himself to be stopped on the road by the onerous conditions of a life in confrontation with sin. He comes to share our existential situation, but he has no part with sin. This incarnation-participation renders possible the perfect expression of the love the Father has for the human race and the perfect human response to this love. Therefore, in our situation, Jesus, animated by the Holy Spirit, manifests the power and the saving love of the Father, and he loves the Father with perfect fidelity, remaining obedient and loving in all his trials, even to death itself. Thus, he reestablishes humanity in the response the Father expects from it. He brings into the world, as a counterweight to scandal, the living witness and the testimony of his fidelity to God.

He transforms our existence, for by sharing in his charity our freedom is rendered more capable of responding to God in charity. And by the presence of the Church in the world (on this earth) the "world" in which Evil reigns no longer constitutes our unique social environment. Therefore, Christ redeems us from a situation made unfavorable by sin, and introduces us to a situation made favorable by the active presence of his love. Jesus, acting as our Head in the name of all men, goes before us on the existential path where we are all called to walk with him. He acts, so as to make us sharers in his situation, that is, so that we may love with him, be animated by his Spirit, already on this earth faithful in trial, and later on in heaven in the communion of the life of glory.

To sum up: *Christ* effects our redemption because *he has come to share our situation,* marred by sin and its consequences, and he has marked it with the sign of fidelity to the Father. He has, therefore, transformed it, and *he has made us capable henceforth of sharing in his situation* which is that of salvation.

This is what the theology of the Greek Fathers held: (*ho ên esôsen*) *he saved what he was.* It is what our contemporaries express in terms that emphasize the movement of the inter-personal dialogue. It is what Scripture tells us by putting the redemption under the sign of the Passover.

For the assistance of catechists who may desire *a great choice of terminology emphasizing the paschal meaning of the redemption,* we will close with a somewhat extensive list of these expressions:

Jesus has shared our earthly life; he died and rose from the dead for us.

He accomplished and continues to accomplish our redemption. He has redeemed us; he makes us free, by being the first to pass through all the obstacles created by sin.

He 'takes away' our sin whose painful consequences he has 'borne'. He saves us; he delivers us; he makes us participants in the salvation he brings to us, notably in the New Covenant he establishes.

He reestablishes us in union with God; he reconciles us to God.

He makes us enter into the kingdom of God, into light, into life.

He repairs and restores our life of union with God; he re-orients us to God.

He draws us after him to the Father; he brings us back to the Father.

He makes us pass from sin to sanctification, from death to life.

He transforms us (us, our existence, our vital existential situation, our life).

Having lived out our life even to death in fidelity to God, Jesus now lives with the Father.

From heaven he sends us his Spirit, to make us capable of living, dying, and rising from the dead in participation with his obedience to, and his love for, the Father and all men.

4. *Catechesis and the "Spirituality of the Redemption"*

It is not enough to give an exposition of the mystery of the redemption in a valid terminology and according to a synthesis that groups all the essential elements. It is also necessary for each subject in catechesis to be treated while taking into account this mystery that is the essential nucleus of revelation. This is why the (dialectical) movement of the redemption must have a place, more or less explicit as the circumstances require, in all catechesis.

This can be done in a three-pronged approach:

(a) *Orienting* the plane of nature with respect to the plane of the supernatural. In this first phase natural and supernatural truths as well as values will be posited, rather vaguely, as prolongations of each other, in *continuity*

(b) *Confronting* the two planes with each other and emphasizing their *discontinuity*.

A double rupture is then presented, without destroying all unity, but making apparent the need for a change in perspective, since the higher plane is something "other", different in its relation to the inferior. The latter must be brought into relation with, and limited by, the former; that is, *detachment* is required. It is difficult for man to accept the fact that his spontaneous desires for unimpeded development which will permit the realization, pure and simple, of natural values, will not be effected.

In fact, man does not always accept this detachment. So he introduces a new source of trouble into his situation, namely *sin.* A further rupture with the system of values takes place, within the sinner himself (an increase in his evil tendencies) as well as in the world, where the opposition of sinners becomes manifest.

This second phase implies, therefore, the necessity for continuing personal *conversion,* and the need for an apostolate, directed to the struggle against "the sin that is in the world".

(c) *Integrating* the two planes with each other, according to a purified conception of their unity, that of *transcendence* in view of a more perfect commitment. Unity, which was vague in the first phase, becomes distinct in the third, for it is the fruit of purification and of a point of view that goes beyond the mere prolongation of natural truths and values. This transcendence includes also a perspective, in which the full realization of supernatural values and of the natural values accepted by the Christian, will be accomplished only after death, being radical detachment. The full realization will not be simply the result of human effort, even when supported by divine grace, but will be a new gift of God.

Realizations effected here below will then appear sometimes as the anticipation of, sometimes as preparation for, the Christian eschatology.

In each phase of this approach catechetical method will bring in one aspect of the "paschal" action of *Christ's redemption:* incarnation—cross—resurrection.

CHAPTER IV

FURTHER EXAMINATION OF CERTAIN ELEMENTS OF THE SYNTHESIS

I. MEANING OF EXPIATION IN THE WRITINGS OF THE PROPHETS

The term had first a ritual sense: the accomplishment of a rite of expiation-purification, in order to banish the state of guilt. (At the beginning, as we have said, there was no clear distinction made between the guilt as the result of a voluntary transgression and incurred "legally", even by an involuntary act.) The danger consisted in thinking that rites could replace the dispositions of the heart. It is against this error that the prophets react.

God does not want ritual offerings that "replace" the man's good dispositions; he wants *the heart of man*. Sin is an infidelity of the heart. It is the heart of man that must return to God. Chastisement falls only on the guilty man in order to bring about his conversion.

Expiation-purification has a double aspect. On man's side it is some painful work (the acceptance of suffering related to the sin) carried out with a view to turning from sin, opening the self to God's pardon and having a "new heart". But this new heart is itself a gift of God. Thus, on God's side, expiation-purification consists in bringing to bear the force of his love that purifies and transforms the heart of men.

It is remarkable that it is a single prophet, Ezekiel, who, during his exile, clarified the spiritual meaning and the personalist meaning of salvation.

"The soul that sinneth, the same shall die . . . The son shall not bear the iniquity of the father, and the father shall not bear the iniquity of the son. . . . Is it my will that a sinner should die, saith the Lord God, and not that he should be converted from his ways, and live?" (Ez. 18, 4. 20. 23). "And I will give you a new heart, and put a new spirit within you. . . . and they shall know that I am the Lord" (Ez. 36, 26. 38). "Behold, I will send spirit into you, and you shall live" (Ez. 37, 5).

What interpretation can properly be given to the sufferings of one who is not personally guilty before God? And above all, what meaning is there in *the persecutions that sinners inflict on God's elect* because of the fidelity he shows in carrying out his mission? for example, Jeremiah, and perhaps also the author of the second part of the Book of Isaiah? This is the crucial question to which an answer, still a very mysterious one, is given in the songs of the *Servant of Yahweh*. A new synthesis is here sketched out, although it still makes use of expressions borrowed from an outlook that it has already left behind. Therefore, it will be necessary to avoid interpretations that would be regressive, and we must try to understand the whole in its different parts in the sense corresponding to the development of revelation, namely, in a sense at once personalist and communal. This understanding is "realistic" with respect to the psychological and corporal setting in which man is placed, and "spiritual" with respect to the union that obtains between the salvific action of God and the action of his elect, the living instrument of salvation.

We may try, therefore, to respond with the proper shades of meaning to the three questions asked concerning the "Servant of Yahweh": What specially marked his existence; what is the reality of the life behind the expressions employed by the author? What person is indicated by the term *Servant?* What is the meaning of his sufferings and his glorification?

These three questions are closely interwoven. Reflecting on the principal verses of Chapters 42, 49, and 53 of Isaiah, and admitting that the possible diversity of persons intended does not exclude a certain unity, we will bring forth factors that will provide the elements to answer the three questions at one and the same time.

(a) Is. 42, 1–7: The *Servant* is the elect of God; not directly a victim, but a man invested with the power of God. Upon the Servant rests *the Spirit* (v. 1) which renders him capable to proclaim the word of God and to "bring forth the prisoners out of prison" (v. 7). This man will carry out his mission with meekness and fidelity (vv. 3–4).

(b) Is. 49, 1–6: The *Servant* is he—the true Israel —in whom Yahweh will glory (v. 3) and by whom the salvation of Yahweh will reach to all the nations of the earth (v. 6). Certain commentators who find it difficult to reconcile the collective sense of v. 3 with an individual sense in vv. 5–6, propose to consider the *Israel* of v. 3 as a gloss. This is not necessary when one knows how close are the bonds between the individual-as-type and the group.

In the Semitic mind, both are here in question, namely, one *by* the other: Israel is the entire nation, called to be the Servant of Yahweh, for the salvation of all men. When Israel as a whole is unfaithful, it is the faithful "remnant" which constitutes the true Israel, and the remnant comes to a focus in the person who represents it. The relation between the representative par excellence and the group does not constitute a substitution of one instead of the other, but a solidarity in vocation and a communion in fidelity. We should note that in Is. 42 and 49 (the same is true of Is. 53) certain characteristics of the Servant bring us face to face with a man who has a *prophetic mission,* while others are signs of a *royal mission.*

(c) Is 53, 1–12: The *Servant* is now an object of contempt; he is a man of sorrows; he is thought to be chastized by God; he suffers because of our sins, he is dumb as a lamb led to the slaughter; he is put to death; he offers up his life; he receives the most complete blessing: light, life, justification of the multitude, overlordship.

The expressions are traditional and without nuances. Thus, v. 6: "The Lord hath laid on him the iniquity of us all" reminds us of texts like "He shall bear his iniquity" (Lev. 5, 1, etc.), that is, he shall bear the punishment for it, and "We have borne the iniquities of our fathers" (Lam. 5, 7). However, since the time of Ezekiel we know that it is not the sin itself of which an innocent man is made to bear the guilt, and that the sufferings of the just man are not a chastisement for *him:* there is no such thing as pure collective culpability, or, above all, substitution. In fact, it is nowhere affirmed that God "transfers" the sin or the punishment from one to another. But the just man may have to undergo the effects (whether actual or subsequent) of the sins of which others are guilty.

Suffering and death, which the just man undergoes in persecution, have for him, therefore, a meaning different from what they have for the guilty. What God expects of his Servant is not that he should pay the debt of other men (again, no mention is made anywhere either of debt or of payment), what is emphasized, on the contrary, is that the Servant accomplished his mission in the meekness of *fidelity* in the midst of *trials*. The figures of the lamb and the sheep directly signify this meekness. We may note that it is a question of a lamb led to the slaughter (not to sacrifice) parallel with a sheep which lets itself be sheared (not with a view to bring offered in this case, either).

However, these images will later be linked with the image of the gift "in *sacrifice* for sin", the sin-offering (*asham*). Here again we are not dealing with a tribute fixed by some law of equivalence, but with a *gift* that has an *intercessory* value for sinners. This sacrificial gift is nothing other than *this same fidelity in trial*. And the end to be reached by intercession consists in this complex reality which is "salvation": God's strength that helps sinners to be converted, the conversion of sinners, divine pardon, cessation of punishment, and the return of blessing in every order of being.

That this is the real nature of things we perceive in the *conclusion* of the songs of the Servant. These are the verses that present the greatest difficulty, first for the translator, for the manuscripts contain many texts, and then for the commentator who seeks to determine the meaning. The Servant receives a prolongation of his life which permits him to see the light: is this the face of God in the light of the Temple? He is permitted to finish his mission, which for a time was interfered with. Once this mission is finished, it means the salvation of a multitude of his people and even the entrance of the nations into the kingdom that God confides to him.

How did the prophet's hearers understand this "length of days after death"? If we limit ourselves to seeing the Servant as a single individual, the difficulty is very great. L. Richard says very prudently: "Exegetes hesitate to see in verse 11, taken literally, the announcement of the resurrection of the Lord. This would be a most unusual anticipation, three centuries before Daniel, when the certainty of this hope will be stated".[4] Must we have recourse to beliefs like the one which would see Elizah escaping death and destined to return so as to finish his mission? But Jesus will tell his disciples that Elizah has already come. It was not necessary to expect to see him again in person; he was to be recognized in him who concluded the mission of the prophets.

The mind of the Semite saw no separation between the group and the persons who successively represented the group. "While remaining an individual, the suffering Servant of the fourth song, in virtue of the oscillation so characteristic of Hebrew thought, truly represents the nation whose mission he carries out in a truly unique degree," says J. De Fraine on this point.[5]

Therefore, it seems more in conformity with his mentality to see the Servant in relation to the fidelity or infidelity of the whole people: faithful Israel, persecuted by the unfaithful Israel, becomes the instrument

---

[4] L. Richard, *Le Mystère de la Redemption* (Tours: Desclée, 1959), p. 32.

[5] J. De Fraine, *Adam and the Family of Man* (New York: Alba House).

of salvation for the return of all to fidelity, and even for the entrance of the nations into the kingdom. He is the survivor of the "remnant", who will be once again, whether *group* or *Servant,* charged with representing the group.

Conclusion

The texts on expiation, and especially those which concern the Servant of Yahweh, are to be interpreted in their context; the context will throw light on the double meaning of expiation-purification and the intrinsic relationship that exists between the mission, prophetic and royal at once, of the Servant and his sufferings.

(1) The expiatory and purifying value of *the blood* comes from its sacred character. It is God who designates it as an instrument of reconciliation. But he supposes an "openness" on the part of the sinner who desires his own conversion.

Suffering as such and death as loss of life in this world have no "power to reconcile". They are intended to make man better disposed, that is, to bring him to regret his sin and open his heart to God's pardon.

The acceptance of punishment by the guilty man has the value of supplication: through it he asks pardon for himself. Its acceptance by the just man, the assuming of suffering which is related to the sin of another (acceptance in fidelity and love) has intercessory value for the guilty.

The sacrificial rite accomplished for them is also a form of intercession.

(2) There is an intrinsic relationship between *the prophetic function* of the Servant and his sufferings. The whole history of the "servants", and especially that of

the prophets, furnishes us with the proper context in which to see these sufferings: they are caused by the hearers who are dissatisfied with the message brought by the prophet. The sufferings of the Servant are not simply natural misfortunes, nor are they difficulties he meets with outside of his role as preacher. Death is inflicted upon him by those who do not wish to hear his message. His mission does not consist in reducing his preaching to a certain time-span, and then submitting to his sufferings, as if they were two different segments of his life; his unique mission is to be faithful unto death in the witness that God requires him to give. And what is obtained by this fidelity-unto-death is precisely that the same witness may be proclaimed with an even greater force, and that the Lord gives efficacious salvation to those who receive it.

Therefore, the cause of, as well as the efforts to bring about, the death of the Servant of Yahweh are found to be in intrinsic relationship with the faithful proclamation of the action God is carrying out in his people, and with the rejection or faithful acceptance of this action of God as it is manifested by his Servant.

II. THE MEANING OF THE DEATH OF CHRIST

The meaning and the value of *the death of Jesus on the cross* must be interpreted by taking explicitly into account the "situation" in which this death took place. For this situation belongs to the event itself. It makes up the context in which it is necessary to read the text.

The bloody death of Jesus takes place in a situation that proves to be the ultimate act of fidelity to the witness of love which it is his mission to give—an act out of which Jesus makes the perfect sacrificial act of expiation and communion. It is a bloody death, brought on, not by a natural cause, but by *the violence of those who refuse his message*.

This violence, moreover, is not experienced in an interior attitude of revolt, but it is *assumed* freely by Jesus as "situation" for *the accomplishment of the mission* to which he has been actively faithful all through his life.

The essential elements of this "situation" consist in the connection existing between the fact of the death and (a) the events preceding it; (b) the events accompanying it; (c) and those following it. Moreover, these elements are emphasized by certain words of Jesus himself.

(a) The cross has *an intrinsic relationship with the events preceding it*. The public life of the Messiah formed the living proclamation of the kingdom of God, and the definitive revelation of the mission the Father had entrusted to Jesus. The kingdom of God is the kingdom of love: love of God and love for men, love of men for each other; universal love, even for enemies, because such is the love of God for men; love that requires detachment from the goods of this world.

Christ has been made king after the manner of this kingdom, as ambassador of the Father, not on a political plane, but on the religious plane. Jesus is the messenger, the prophet of his own function as royal head. But this function does not coincide with two points in the mentality of his hearers. On the one hand, it is less than what they are expecting of the Messiah: Christ is not a king-liberator of the political order; on the other, it is more than the Pharisees will accept in a man: Jesus declares that he is the Son, having all things in common with the Father, that to receive the Son and his life is to receive the true messianic riches promised by God, and that the Son has the power to communicate his life as the supreme gift of God.

The crowd, superficial as all crowds are, is not interested in a Messiah who does not bring them earthly riches, and, in particular, national independence: they choose Barabbas, the revolutionary, in preference to Jesus who brings them directly only a spiritual kingdom.

The pharisees, more skilled in discovering the profound meaning of the declarations of Jesus on the matter of his divine prerogatives, have him condemned as a blasphemer.

If Jesus had denied his teaching, his royal mission and his divine prerogatives, he would not have had to suffer the effects of popular disappointment, pharasaic indignation, and the cowardice of a foreign judge, anxious not to displease Caesar.

But in the course of his trial Jesus affirms, on the contrary, in the clearest possible manner his message and this mission which, rejected by men, become *the reasons for the condemnation of Jesus;* and it is as based on these reasons that Jesus accepts his death as the supreme testimony to the veracity of the message and the mission.

(b) Among *the circumstances of the death itself* which emphasize its meaning, we select three, moreover, related to one another: the violent suffering caused by the enemies of his mission, the hostility of those to whom he came to testify his love, and the impression he has of being abandoned by his Father. It is these three elements that give evidence of the perfect fidelity of Jesus to his mission.

When God's will for us comprises suffering, we experience the temptation either to adopt the fatalist attitude of one who must undergo what he cannot avoid though he finds what is happening to him absurd, or to rebel, accusing God because he has not spared us. Is our fidelity proof against temptation? Jesus, who entered into participation with our earthly condition because of the Father's will, knows our trials. On the cross he experiences suffering of the highest degree, the suffering of death felt as a radical and frightfully painful tearing. It is the final *trial* resulting from the condition brought into the world by the disobedience of men. Jesus remains faithful in this test of *submission* and *humility,* finding his strength in the will of the Father.

He does not lapse either into a blind fatalism or into a bitter revolt, but he freely accepts the Father's accomplishment of the Father's will in him, and that he gives him the strength to remain faithful to this end. Jesus shows himself faithful to that obedience lived in the full *consciousness of the meaning* of this trial: his obedience becomes the force which will triumph over the disobedience of men; his acceptance of this death is the victory won by him over death, and not only for himself, but for all those who will be united to him.

This same will of the Father, which makes Jesus a sharer in our earthly lot, intends that he shall thus practice charity among men. Jesus also remains faithful to love for men in *the trial that is the most acute for this love.* Where so many others have turned away with bitterness in the face of ingratitude and the hostility of those to whom they only wished to do good, Jesus practices to perfection *the love of his enemies,* even asking the Father to forgive them. He is not thinking of himself, he has in view only the conversion of those who, up to this time, have not yet received the light he has brought them.

His fidelity in trial is most admirable with respect to

his trust of the Father. And here *the test* touches on a mystery that remains very dark to us. What was the experience of Jesus on the cross, his impression of abandonment by the Father, coupled with his confidence in the Father? The torment he endured in the Garden of Olives was doubtless felt in all its acuteness on the cross. Humanly speaking, Jesus desires to be delivered in all haste as quickly as possible from these horrible sufferings of the senses and the heart. But this "cup" will not depart from him until he has drained it to the lees; and he knows that the Father will also give him the strength to do so.

Psalm 21, which expresses in such touching fashion the dismay before "the silence of God", is entirely appropriate to what Jesus experienced in realizing that his sufferings had not been shortened by a special intervention of his Father. He felt this "distance" all the more as his enemies challenged him. He called himself the one sent by God, God's favorite, come to save Israel. If he told the truth, let the protection of God be shown, let it begin by delivering him!

The greatest trial for any man is certainly the one that appeals to trust in the midst of an impression of abandonment. In giving voice to the cry of Psalm 21, Jesus expresses this feeling; and no doubt he used the end of this psalm to testify his loyal confidence to the Father. In any case, this is shown, joined to the total gift of self, in the final words of Jesus when dying: "Father, into thy hands I commend my spirit."

Jesus offers this fidelity in trial as a sacrifice. Fidelity, which is charity toward men out of *love* for God; fidelity which is *trust,* and *obedience* because it is exactly what the Father expects as a response. Supreme fidelity because witnessed to in the supreme test. Fidelity witnessed to *in the name of all men,* for Jesus is the true Israel, "representing" all the new, chosen people to whom will belong all who are truly united to Jesus. Fidelity which is *the sacrifice of expiation* because Jesus offers it in intercession for the forgiveness of our sins. Fidelity, finally, which will be finished eternally in the *sacrifice of communion,* as is shown in the relation between the cross and the resurrection.

(c) *The bond between the death of Jesus and his glorious life* is so close, so intrinsically essential, that it makes of them two sides of a unique reality, namely, the reality which is the "hour" of Jesus. In this hour Jesus passed out of this world to the Father. He who had come from the bosom of the Father returned to the Father by the road the Father had traced out for him.

This "passage" which is in reality his *sacrifice of communion,* Jesus not only had knowledge of, so that he could consciously accept it, but he had it within his power. He had received from his Father, at the same time as his mission, the power "to lay down his life and to take it up again". He can dispose of his life according to the intentions of the Father. And this is what he does in his return to the Father by the way of the cross, which thus becomes the initial step in his sacrifice of communion.

Having received this power as redeemer of men, Jesus can promise to associate them with his communion. He does so in assuring the good thief that on that very day he will be with him in paradise. The final words of Jesus are the expression of the gift by which he enters fully into communion with his Heavenly Father.

The life of glory is nothing else but the eternal crown

of this sacrificial communion. Jesus entered into the glory where the Father was awaiting him, and where he welcomed him with the gift of that same glory. And he has the power to have us enter into communion with God.

He does so by sending the Spirit of the Father and the Son; he will do so finally when all men will have passed through death to share with him his own eternal glory. These two complementary aspects are together symbolized in "the pierced side, from which flowed the blood and water". They appear together again in the symbol of the Lamb "standing, slain", as the Apocalypse shows him.

Jesus himself reveals his mission and the manner in which he fulfills it, in his words and deeds. And it is the indissoluble unity of his "hour", freely lived in his "situation", which shows us in definitive form the sense in which Jesus effects our redemption.

III. THE MEANING OF OUR SUFFERINGS IN THE ECCLESIAL COLLABORATION WITH THE REDEMPTIVE WORK OF CHRIST

For the interpretation of the biblical context, especially of St. Paul, we draw chiefly from an article by L. Lochet, which we warmly recommend,[6] and to which we add the commentary of the famous passage of the Epistle of St. Paul to the Colossians (1, 24). We will then develop an application of it which is valid for every Christian.

1. *Context of St. Paul's Statements*

Life in general, the life of the Christian in particular

[6] L. Lochet, "Pénitence et vie apostolique," in *Christus* X (1963) n. 39, pp. 368–85.

and the life of the apostle in a still more special way, gives us the experience of joy and suffering. For St. Paul, difficulties should rouse our trust in God, since they make it possible for us to show forth the power and goodness of God. This very confidence then becomes a source of joy.

The apostle, devoted to the service of Christ in his brothers, will meet with suffering, not simply in a certain austerity that he will impose upon himself to fit himself for the apostolate, but above all in the exercise of the apostolate itself. For he experiences within himself the trials of other men, and, at the same time, he rejoices in their joy (2 Cor. 2, 4; 7, 4; 11, 28; Phil. 2, 2; 3, 18; Col. 2, 5). It is, therefore, his communion with other men that furnishes him with the content of his trials and his joys.

This communion is of such a nature that the action of the apostle has an effect on the community. All that he does "for" the Church (his preaching, his journeys, etc.) and the whole experience of tribulation and consolation that he acquires in this activity, are of profit to the Church; his suffering is the suffering of childbirth; it conditions the birth and the growth of the Christian communities for which he labors (Gal. 4, 19; Eph. 3, 13). In a special way the experience of joy (the offspring of which is trust) in the midst of tribulation permits him to console those who are afflicted.

But this communion has a still deeper and even more profound dimension: it is a communion with Jesus Christ. It is not simply psychological and practical on the human plane; it integrates human communion, and animates it with a higher life, by participation in the mystery of Christ. This mystery is the ontological and active union that exists between Christ and ourselves.

What has been done, what is still being done in the Head, is done more and more in the members. The cross and the resurrection of Jesus become a shared reality in the trials and in the joys that are caused by our union with him and by our collaboration with his testimony (2 Cor. 4, 8–12). The author we have cited concludes: "This is the fact we have to deal with, and this alone: the mystery of Christ, the paschal mystery in us and through us . . . Sharing in the passion of Christ in the very sufferings inherent in his ministry, the apostle enters by this road into his resurrection and this mystery in him becomes a source of life for all men." [7]

This context, completed by a certain shade of meaning which we intend to point out, allows us to interpret correctly the often discussed text of Colossians 1, 24–25. St. Paul, now in prison, speaks of the sufferings that he will still have to endure; they are sufferings that are inflicted upon him because he preaches Christ; and this preaching is the basis of the service that he renders as one of the ministers of the Church. The genitive *"of Christ"* which determines what is lacking of the sufferings, is, therefore, not subjective but objective: what is in question here is not some lack in the sufferings of Christ that he will have to make up, but of other, and still-to-be-endured sufferings that are inflicted on Paul *for Christ's sake*. All of this has direct bearing, therefore, on what has just been laid down as the general context in St. Paul's writings. The supplementary nuance comes from a context that is also to be found more than once in St. Paul: that of an exchange of joy as of deficiencies, between him and his Christians.

The joy of his Christians, communicated to Paul,

[7] *Loc. cit.,* p. 379.

make up for his afflictions; and the spiritual riches that Paul can communicate to them make up for their deficiencies. Thus, in the first Epistle to the Thessalonians: "For what thanks can we return to God for you for all the joy wherewith we rejoice for your sakes before our God? Night and day we pray more and more that we may see you again, and may supply those things that are lacking to your faith" (1 Thess. 3, 9–10). It is the same context which we find in Colossians 1, 4 (again in verse 8) and 9: "We give thanks to the God and Father of our Lord Jesus Christ . . . for we have heard of your faith in Christ Jesus and of the love that you bear towards all the saints . . . This is why we too have been praying for you unceasingly, since the day we heard this, and asking that you may be filled with knowledge of his will, in all spiritual wisdom and understanding".

The beginning of verse 24 corresponds to the first part of this exchange: "I rejoice now in the sufferings I bear for your sake." The translations usually link the end of the member with *sufferings,* but it can also be referred to *I rejoice* (cf. verses 4 and 8). The remainder of verse 24 corresponds to the return movement: it begins, in fact, in a characteristic manner with some prefixes, which the Vulgate has not translated: *"ant-, ana-, plero-,* I rejoice now in the sufferings I bear for your sake; and what is lacking of the sufferings of Christ (for Christ's sake) I fill up in my flesh for his body, which is the Church."

The verse which immediately follows makes clear the cause of the sufferings which he is speaking about: they are the sufferings which Paul finds in his ministry of the Church "whose minister I have become in virtue of the office that God has given me in your regard. For I am to preach the world of God fully". Once again, we are here in contact with the general context of the primitive tradition.

2. *Sufferings and Joys in the Life of Every Apostolic Christian*

Even if we prescind from any special apostolic orientation, *all progress in charity* is a collaboration in the redemptive work of Christ, to the benefit of its immediate author as well as to his brethren. Every joy and every suffering, with the exception of those that are sought from evil motives, can become the occasion of an active attitude of charity. But what is the relationship between suffering and a specific apostolic orientation?

Suffering does not constitute a kind of spiritual fund that we must endeavor to increase in order to buy souls. Souls are not for sale. The redemptive action consists in fidelity to love, especially in what concerns the proclamation of God's intervention. In certain circumstances and for different reasons, this practice of charity will be conditioned by suffering. Thus, suffering will have a certain value in an apostolic life. First of all, the apostle will always have to struggle against sin in his own life. All *mortification* sanely motivated by resistance to the disorder still at work within ourselves, will be translated into an improvement in our apostolic "witness".

In apostolic activity we will be speaking either of the practice of abnegation, or of bearing unsought trials, rather than of pentitential mortifications. Suffering will be present in four forms, namely: the difficulties natural to apostolic work; fasting, or its equivalent; apostolic concern properly so-called, resulting from participation in the spiritual needs of our neighbor; and persecution, which, in fact, will appear in vastly different forms. We have already said a few words on each of these sufferings, which are the conditioning of apostolic charity (see page 92f.). It may be helpful here to insist on *the relationship that exists between these modes of abnegation or trial and the twofold availability proper to the apostle.*

When the disciples whom Jesus had sent out on a mission met with an obstacle, he recalled them to the necessity for prayer and fasting. If, to speak in general terms, fasting (or the voluntary privation of the enjoyment of created things) serves prayer, this is particularly true of "an apostolic fast", that is, the apostle must believe in and must manifest the divine origin of all redemptive activity. He prays because it is from God that apostolic efficacy comes; he detaches himself in some measure from the use of creatures, even as a means of apostolic action, as a "sign" that he is at the service of the work that God wills to carry out even with poor means, namely, the witness of evangelical virtues and the word. In the same way, the detachment the apostle practices is directed toward his service of men to whom his word is addressed. He strips himself of material goods in the measure in which they create a regrettable distance between him and his brethren. He will above all strip himself of interior attitudes that are too narrow; for example, he will rid himself of chauvinism so that he may enter into an ever greater communication, both human and Christian, with all other men.

Therefore, everything comes back to love: it is charity which is the source; its manifestation is the message; its way of entering into communication is the fundamental mode of the redemptive action of Jesus and of our collaboration with his work.

Just as a free man who wants to liberate a prisoner might come to seek him in the place of his captivity, share with him the difficulties of his situation, and might take him with him into freedom, so Christ, the ambassador of the Father, came to seek us in our captivity, without ever himself being guilty of sin. *Jesus has shared our earthbound condition, even to its most wearisome aspects, so that we might become sharers in his liberating strength even here below, and in total freedom for a glorious eternity. This participation is a mode of action realized by a life lived in communion;* this liberating strength is the faithful love which is the response to God's invitation to us. *In just the same way the apostles, in whom and by whom Christ continues his work in his Church,* must be faithful witnesses to the charity of God.

Unlike Jesus, they will first of all have to become converted and continue the struggle against sin in their own members. But afterward, in conformity with Jesus, the witness of their charity must be made flesh by participation in the situation of those men to whom the Lord sends them. And they will do so in the measure that they are at the service of God and man, in the measure that they bring to all men "the word of God in truth".

This conformity with Christ Jesus is no mere external likeness. It is the working-out of our existential participation in the very love of Christ in his redemptive work. For this reason we share in his sufferings and his joys, and in the latter, not solely because we are looking forward to the life in glory, but because already here on earth we have the experience of the love and trust that are the sources of the deepest and richest joy.

CHAPTER V

A CONTEMPORARY EXPLANATION OF HUMAN CONDITIONING FACTORS

Situating the problem is fairly complex, for we are dealing in fact with a whole range of questions, namely:

Does a person of a particular psychology, influenced by a given environment, experience a *conscious need* of salvation? It often happens that the awareness of a need lags behind the actual urgency of this need.

What kind of salvation is this need seeking to express? Deliverance from evil and access to the benefits which ensure happiness must be envisaged on different planes. For example, relief from hunger, freedom from anguish, the abolition of slavery, economic affluence, technological power, the individual mastery of passions, effective social organization, mutual understanding among human beings, love of God, the stability afforded by a happy destiny. Relationships exist between these planes. Which relationships appear the most important to a particular mentality?

By what means and following which path can salvation be realized according to this mentality?

In particular, *what role* is accorded to *God* (Providence), to *Jesus Christ,* to the *Church,* that is, to the ecclesiastical institution, to the community of Christians, and to *each man* in relation to this community?—this role envisaged as being both *receptive* and *active* in collaborating toward personal salvation and the salvation of humanity?

A. Psychological Development

A little child normally places his trust in God. Salvation appears as something positive: God makes a promise and the child spontaneously relates the fulfilling of this promise to the idea of a reward meted out to those who obey God's wish. Jesus Christ is God's powerful envoy and he comes to save all those who are unhappy. We should avoid indicating too prematurely that there may be a connection between the cross of Jesus and the child's own failings, but we can in all seriousness point out the fact that certain grown-up people commit very great sins. When the sinner does not halt on the path of sin, he comes to the point of wishing that he will not meet Jesus on the way; he might even wish him to disappear completely from his life. That is why sinners put him to death. But even when Jesus was crucified, he remained good to mankind and obedient to his Father. Since his resurrection, he has continued to help mankind. We can always rely upon him, for he is our Savior, and one day we will be reunited with him in Heaven.

The psychology of a *school child* is responsive to the idea of necessary order and the consequences entailed by breaking away from order; it is therefore responsive to the need for re-establishing order. Accordingly, redemption should be presented to school children in this light. Men, who are sinners, introduce disorder into the world and this disorder increases. God sends forth his Son to place a barrier between us and sin, and to show us how to live according to an order which he wills. The Son proves his own love for God by obeying him unto death upon the cross. When we have sinned, we must listen to the summons of Jesus who invites us to ask God's forgiveness. Jesus gives us the strength to love God and our neighbor according to his example. We must try never to give way anew to bad behavior and to carry out God's wishes with increasing perfection. Thus we shall participate more and more in the happiness that God reserves for us.

Moreover, at this particular age in which children easily acquire data which they understand very incompletely, not only in our subject but in others as well, the teaching they receive on redemption could discreetly impart certain notions and truths, even certain words and expressions, which will later provide the elements of a more developed doctrinal and systematic instruction.

The *adolescent,* on the other hand, is refractory to any notional system one seeks to impose upon him, if this system does not happen to correspond with inner experience, for this first reflective experience of the self is precisely the one which has the most important conditioning effect upon adolescence. But the experience develops in two directions, or rather, in terms of "tension", between two extremes. On the one hand, the adolescent aspires to noble personal realizations and notably to consistency in carrying out moral resolutions which he has formed willingly. On the other hand, he becomes aware that his freedom, as a personal dynamism in the realization of moral values, is very defective. Therefore his main concern is to discover what kind of assistance he can expect from Christ the Savior in the development and stabilizing of his inner life, particularly in the development of the freedom he will devote to good.

More mature adolescents, who have left the stage of psychological introversion behind them, are interested in their relationships with others. As they approach the threshold of adulthood, the social aspects of redemption acquire greater significance.

The *adult,* in the full sense of this word, may be defined as one who has achieved perfect integration both psychologically and in his entire behavior. By this we mean the integration of his own person with all the essential factors of life, and the integration of his person with all the meaningful forms of life shared with others, namely the family, occupation, friendship, etc.

In fact, development within adult life normally follows two different directions that are sometimes divergent, then intersect anew, but are always fundamentally destined to be reunited. These directions are represented on the one hand by the formation of life's exterior conditioning factors, particularly the elaboration of social institutions, and on the other, by interpersonal encounters increasing both in intimacy and in universality. In others words: society (in particular socialization) and the community (in particular mutual personalization): a better world (in particular an improved material framework and greater technological power for "producing" and "organizing") and a more fraternal world (in particular a life based on profound understanding and exhibiting personal sympathy even toward those who are less favored by nature or psychologically more remote); a unification in the sense of physical rapprochement and uniform equalization, and a unification in the sense of a harmony reuniting many complementary aspects and transcending the opposition and petty indifference (races, temperaments, cultures, sociological positions) through integration with a living principle of superior unity.

We must therefore demonstrate the role played by Christ's redeeming action and the role played by the collaboration of mankind in view of a perfect integration. But before outlining the principle points to be emphasized in this type of catechesis, we must pursue our study of conditioning factors one stage further in our examination of the contemporary environment.

B. The Contemporary Mentality

Elsewhere (*The Structure of Catechetics*), we have had occasion to find analogies between contemporary experience and the fundamental data of the Christian message. These analogies allow us to hold a dialogue with modern man on the same wavelength.

It will nevertheless be of some utility to pursue this subject in the present chapter and to center it upon two requirements of the contemporary mentality that are complementary to one another: (1) on the one hand, the experience of autonomy and universal human solidarity; (2) on the other, the need for realism in thought and action; (3) a completely positive answer requires a dynamic synthesis.

1. The search for human *autonomy* can of course be traced, in some way or other, among all nations and at all times. In its present form, it stems from an *experience of development,* namely, the rise of the positive sciences that consider themselves to be autonomous in their own sphere and in their equally autono-

mous application to technology. This explication is made in view of producing earthly benefits which yield a certain satisfaction to mankind.

Everything that contradicts this autonomy and its normal result is henceforth regarded by modern man as an "alienation". As an illustration of this fact: when faced with shortage of food or accommodation, he provides for these contingencies by means of his labor; when faced with sickness, he combats the latter by means of hygiene and medicine; when partly deprived of the fruits of his labor, he counteracts by waging a class struggle; he substitutes democracy for the heteronomy of a political power; he remedies interior conflicts stemming from psychic complexes by medical treatment and eventually by psychoanalysis.

According to this aspect of the contemporary mentality, man finds his negative salvation in progressive liberation from the alienations that still hold him in thrall: his positive salvation in the conquest of human autonomy; his principal means of salvation in science, technology and the *organizing of universal collaboration;* his definite salvation in the indefinite development of the happy result he can effect from generation to generation by his own efforts.

How does this type of man envisage religion?

Religion may interest him from a psychological or social point of view if he deems it capable of fostering inner peace and exterior order, and even if it appears to promise exceptional human realizations, notably at a level superior to his own.

However, we must bear in mind that scientific man holds little sympathy with the mysterious nature of religion.

The man given to earthly enjoyment, which is centered upon itself, encounters several difficulties when faced with the question of religious salvation. In the first place, the fascination exercised by purely human values renders him indifferent or blind to religious values. Moreover, the lure of the sensational and the exciting easily allows him to fall prey to religious deviations, which means in fact that religion, as he experiences it, is occasionally reduced to the possibility of some strange enjoyment. But a third and even greater difficulty awaits him, for he is quick to denounce those aspects of religion which appear to him as alienations, namely, the expectation of heaven that hinders the perfect fulfillment of earthly tasks, religious power that poaches upon the autonomy of the free individual or of civil groups. Finally, man who sets up his own autonomy—and if not his strength at least his constructive tendencies—as an absolute, affirms that God is but a projection into the unreal infinite of that which belongs entirely to man in reality.

This anthropocentric inclination is not of course the only path followed by modern man, as we shall presently demonstrate, but we must grant that *the temptation of atheism based on human (social) self-sufficiency* is a very obvious one. The man who gives way to this movement of pride (whether he realizes its true nature or otherwise) adopts the attitude *of not expecting his salvation from the hands of God but from man,* particularly from the development of positive science and organization. If men choose to live by their own efforts and for themselves, there can be no connection between God and their salvation.

Fortunately *a more complete experience* allows us to see that this pride affords no solution to the problem of man's salvation. Technological and social development, in fact, includes not only its positive elements but also a *negative aspect*. Its inability to ensure man's well-being stems from three causes corresponding to the three levels of man and to the influence exercised by the superior upon the inferior levels.

In the first place, technological development always remains ambivalent when considered on the plane of human values: it can serve to promote man or to oppress and destroy him. The advantages of socialization often go hand in hand with the disadvantages of being englobed by the masses.

Secondly, on the plane of moral order, both individual and social, modern man also experiences his inability, which is relative, but nonetheless profound and continuous, to recognize fully where goodness lies and to practice it faithfully in relation to his own conscience.

Finally, and most important of all, it is equally true that man aspires to transcend earthly values and to unite with someone who offers a remedy to all human imperfections, not only in view of joyfully experiencing love which is superior to man but also in his need to be forgiven after committing a fault that he regrets.

When based on this more complete experience, *the question of religion* reappears in another kind of psychological conditioning. In considering the role of religion in relation to human needs, we must avoid oversimplification. A valid synthesis requires subtlety and discrimination. (See Chap. III.) However, some of its major elements may already be pointed out at this stage.

Jesus Christ delivers man from his false self-sufficiency.

He awakens his sense of superior values and achieves this by immediate reference to God.

He summons man to a conversion, namely to detachment from his overexaggerated confidence in the benefits of this world or in human power, envisaged as sources of happiness.

He grants spiritual enlightenment to those who do not cling obstinately to their own blindness. He bears witness which is both accessible and transcendental to a life lived entirely for God and with God, a life which incorporates in this love of God the fullest extent of love for mankind. He offers himself as an existential (and therefore more than psychological) source of light and strength, of forgiveness and new life.

2. The second *requirement* of the mentality we are seeking to examine concerns *realism of thought and action.*

In seeking its own happiness, this type of mentality has no illusions about man's powers and remains completely clear-sighted on the subject of human defects. Neither is it pessimistic from the outset for it believes that man's potentialities can progress.

If it responds to "complete realism", it can be directly related to our recent statements concerning Christ, for entire realism seeks support from all true advocates, and therefore from Christ likewise, in its desire to remedy human imperfections.

However, if this need for realism is equally situated in an anthropocentric context, it will result, in its own way, in another kind of atheism. Realism of thought is in fact well aware of man's many shortcomings in his attempts to secure happiness: modern man seeks lucidity; he does not entertain the dream of an earthly paradise which would be the result of human effort. The realistic man is equally ready to acknowledge his need of God's assistance. But a realistic mentality formed by the positive and technical sciences expects divine assistance to be embodied in results not only effective from the point of view of man's earthly happiness but also verifiable.

Experience, however, often proves disappointing from both points of view. If there is a God who is capable of helping man, he does not appear to be much preoccupied with the latter's tangible and earthly well-being. For there are so many catastrophes God does not prevent, so much wretchedness, famine and war among the multitudes, whether they be Christian or otherwise, whether they pray to God or ignore him. Hence the temptation of a *practical atheism,* the atheism of man who, for all practical purposes, *does not expect salvation from God.* This type of atheism adopts two divergent forms, represented either by depression subsiding into *fatalistic resignation,* or by *active rebellion* that is equally born of despair but remains determined to employ all human means in its attempt to salvage, without God's aid, as much human happiness as possible. In short, this last form links up with the attitude typified by self-sufficient atheism; but instead of extolling the illusion of perfect happiness that human powers can ensure, this particular atheism counsels man to be content with the imperfect happiness he is capable of conquering either individually or socially.

In the case of this second temptation of atheism as in the first, a *more complete experience* enables man to extricate himself from the predicament. Despair and lack of trust in God are two failings which do not give sufficient consideration to the *positive contribution* made by the *signs that God gives us of his intervention* on behalf of man.

The synthesis will provide a more complete answer

to the difficulty we have just raised. It should stress the actual role played by Christians in relation to these "signs" of God. Moreover, their role relies in itself upon Christ's saving action as it is primarily manifested in the Gospels.

Jesus Christ frees men from lack of trust which stems from a more or less concealed *anthropocentricity*.

Throughout his message, he points to the faithfulness with which God demonstrates his goodwill toward mankind and to the necessity of man's submission to God even when his happiness is involved. Jesus even performs miracles that are striking signs of divine intervention. With regard to his miracles, however, we must note that these interventions of God are always situated on two planes. Because of their material nature, the miracles demonstrate that material and physical advantages are in no way excluded from divine providence. Because of their transcendental significance, the miracles teach us to transcend earthly horizons: earthly gifts are symbols of more perfect gifts which are the only ones that matter in the final reckoning. Moreover, even in the time of our Lord, miracles did not instantly suppress all human needs.

This explains why trust, of which Jesus is both the messenger and the pledge, is the fruit of a conversion that is constantly proclaimed as an indispensable necessity. Men must attach a less exclusive importance to earthly benefits and eschatological salvation must be their only absolute goal. This salvation does not impede human progress on earth but it can be attained by one path alone which always, in some way or other, bears the mark of opposition stemming from the forces of evil.

Jesus himself is a living and perfect proof of this trust,

for he remains consistent with it unto the cross. This is precisely the harshest test of confidence in God, his Father.

In his risen life, Jesus represents the perfect guarantee of our own trust, and notably of the confidence with which we await eternal life from God. By sending forth the Holy Spirit, Christ is the source of our inner strength, enabling us to follow with confidence the Christian path of salvation.

3. When we seek to discover the positive significance of Christian salvation for modern man, the complete answer is provided by a *synthesis* of the elements we have just examined separately. This synthesis is *dynamic,* for it does not consist in static equilibrium but in *movement* stemming from the juncture of several *forces.* We are constantly dealing with a *choice* to be made between two opposite orientations which exist in fact, namely, the one relating to *man's transcendence,* through an action of God recognized as such, or the one relating to *man's withdrawal and self-sufficiency,* in his individual life, in society, in earthly enjoyment or, as a matter of topical interest, in the cosmos.

A dynamic synthesis is in keeping with the dynamic nature of human existence, such as it is led with growing consciousness by modern man. The latter considers himself summoned to *commit himself freely to an evolution* proceeding from lesser to greater perfection. This means that he is ceaselessly *called to transcend* the values he has hitherto realized.

We must make a final attempt to define the nature of (I) the revealing and saving action of Christ, (II) the response of man who actively accepts the gospel message and the divine act of salvation, (III) by applying these meanings to the contemporary scene in particular.

I. *The Revealing and Saving Action of Christ*

Christ came among us to bring *both the revelation and the power of definite transcendence* which are gifts of God. The *Coming of the kingdom* coincides with man's salvation as a gift of God.

The miracles and the words of Jesus exhibit a power that is not only of divine origin (a salvation sent from God), but reveals an intention transcending earthly comfort (a gift consisting in union with God). The gospel message, both enacted and spoken, always appears as a transcendental gift communicated through earthly mediations.

But from the beginning of his ministry, and with complete consistency, Jesus points out in which sense his actions must be understood, the valid direction to be pursued by our thoughts and our deeds, the right course to follow in seeking the transcendence to which he summons us and in the fulfillment of which he brings us strength from God.

We must accord greater attention to the Giver who manifests his kindliness than to the earthly gift by which we profit. It is important to attach greater significance to the union established through this mediation between God and man than to the immediate gain ensured by an earthly advantage. In short, the man who benefits from God's goodness is invited to *transcend self-seeking love in order to enter into the love of communion with God.*

A similar transcendence requires *detachment from created possessions,* in the sense that we cannot place our absolute desire in earthly goods, and that we must on the contrary accord a *"relative"* significance to all things that are not of God himself.

And yet our daily experience teaches us that we are

often tempted to live according to an absolute form of anthropocentricity and that we occasionally succumb to this temptation. This explains why transcendence, to which we are summoned by Christ, equally requires a *conversion* through ever renewed attempts. This last point calls for closer examination.

Individual or social anthropocentricity is a natural tendency capable of evolving along diverging paths. That man should be concerned with self-protection or self-development is of course an inborn instinct. That man should also experience moments in which his attention is entirely centered on his own immediate interests is equally natural. If this tendency remains fundamentally receptive to others, and particularly to God, it can develop according to its "relative" significance which is normal. But when this anthropocentricity is developed into an absolute value, and becomes an attitude into which man voluntarily withdraws, in spite of the fact that God invites him to seek transcendence in love, the position it reaches at this point constitutes the very foundation of sin.

Now it is from sin that Christ delivers us. The man who recognizes his fault and repents of it, receives through Christ, God's pardon. Man struggling against sin, receives as a share in Christ's victory, the pledge of final victory. The salvation which Christ brings affects man in the deepest bearings of his existence. He saves us in a positive way by granting us the light and the strength which enable us to participate in his love of God, to discover our happiness thereby in definite union with God and to understand the "relative" significance of all our attachments to created things when compared to this supreme gift.

The temptation to sin is embodied in the "environment" of those who yield to the anthropocentric tendency made absolute and thereby give cause for scandal. Christ *delivers us from the ascendancy of the sinful environment;* the attestation of his faithfulness to God shines forth in our world, for it provides both the reparation or atonement of our sins and an antidote against the fascination that scandal exercises upon us.

This testimony is one which Christ bore "to the last" by dying upon the *cross,* and he has manifested the radiance of the joy he discovered in his faithful union with the Father by his *resurrection.*

This indeed is the essential gospel message, the heart of the "mystery of salvation", the Christian absolute in relation to which all other values must be considered of subsidiary importance.

II. *Man's Positive Response*

Man's positive response to the revelation and the gift of higher life which Christ offers him must therefore be founded upon a disposition to welcome union with God as an absolute value and to accord a relative significance to all earthly mediations.

The operation consisting in making this "relative" assessment has a negative and a positive aspect. Negatively, we must abandon all absolute quests for earthly benefits (and above all turn away from our absolute anthropocentricity); positively, we must "incarnate" our absolute love of God in earthly mediations that are part of our temporal human condition.

In concrete terms, bearing witness to our acceptance of the gospels should consist in a *threefold testimony of faith,* namely, of our faith in God who saves us in Jesus Christ: the testimony of prayer, of poverty and of charity.

Through *prayer* we render our relationship to God explicit. This explicitness stems from our ability to concentrate and meditate upon the signs by which God make his presence known to us. A Christian is primarily one who "knows" Jesus Christ, and who encounters God in Jesus Christ, especially through his sacramental action. Further on in the present chapter, we shall consider which modalities of prayer are particularly suited to modern man.

Through *Christian poverty,* we renounce all "priority" claims to the riches of this world and we accept this renunciation as a pledge of our absolute search for union with God, a search which is always allied to our trust that God will grant us happiness.

Through *evangelical and brotherly love,* we "incarnate" our union with God in the union we achieve with our fellowmen, as a token of the transcendent dynamism that has been imparted to us, for the forms adopted by a Christian's love of his fellowmen transcend instinctive solidarities.

The principle of Christian transcendence relies therefore upon our union with the Father, through Christ who is faithful unto the cross and glorified in his resurrection. This union is in fact the fruit of a *living principle,* namely, the Holy Spirit who is sent forth among us.

This *essential content* of "Christian salvation" and the *fundamental procedure* followed by Christ in the gospels in order to reveal this content and bring about our participation, are the same for all men and remain valid for all times. The *modalities* which correspond to successive stresses on different aspects of the content and to practical ways of realizing this process of participation in the incarnation, the cross and the resurrection, vary nonetheless according to different nations and epochs.

The question of discovering which modalities are best suited to our times is directly related to the subject of *the Church's aggiornamento*. Following the prophetic directive of John XXIII, the Church must in fact "bring herself up to date". The Church must be "the gospel of Jesus Christ, proclaimed and lived today". In order to achieve this, the Church must recognize the modalities of thought, expression and life, which are best suited to her present task, so as to remain clearly and recognizably in reference with the gospels, and in such a way that the testimony she renders to Christ can be made intelligible to all. Once these modalities have been acknowledged, the Church must truly incorporate them into her life, in the midst of the present world, so that all modern values may participate in the salvation which, through Jesus Christ, comes to us from God.

III. *Features of the Contemporary Situation*

Let us attempt to apply this directive to the features of the contemporary situation recently singled out in the present chapter. The question is one of contact between the *gospel of salvation* and *human promotion on worldly planes*.

We have already defined these two terms.

The promotion of humanity in a worldly context links up with our previous reference to the justification on which contemporary needs for autonomy, solidarity and realism are founded.

A sense of autonomy and a sense of universal human collaboration are legitimate acquisitions of the contemporary mentality, provided these are not conceived as absolutes, for religion cannot be a substitute for technological effort or human entente from the point of view of their respective roles in promoting humanity. Similarly, the positive and human sciences rightly affirm that they are "competent" to govern in their own realm.

Ethics and religion must therefore underline the importance of attributing a "relative" significance to these spheres. Ethics coordinates them in the totality of human existence. Religion is concerned with ordering these relatively autonomous spheres of human life in harmony with the relationship existing between God and man, and which constitutes the supreme value.

The gospel of salvation invites us to achieve transcendence, which entails a conversion and a relative realization of earthly values, or rather this transcendence is experienced in two ways, namely, through eschatological anticipation and through the mediation of human values. Responsiveness to Christian transcendence is translated by a threefold form of testimony, represented by prayer, poverty and charity. How can contact between these two terms be established?

Psychologically speaking, it is understandable that the *"spirituality of the incarnation" should primarily attract* Christians in the modern world. They feel the need to envisage Christianity as an extension of human values such as they are experienced today. Now the progress of technology can serve to free man from certain alienations or forms of material servitude, and solidarity in the sphere of work, organization and mutual assistance can provide even more favorable ground for the flowering of charity among human beings. Therefore, the *testimony of Christian charity* primarily appears as the much needed point of contact between the gospels and the modern world. This charity is lived through the "mediations" provided by technological collaboration in view of social justice. It transcends the material enjoyment of society and natural solidarities. By practicing it, Christians equally bear the signs of God's salvation to those who are tempted to give way to despair.

But we cannot remain blind to the *temptation of human self-sufficiency* which easily derives from technological and social development, namely, the temptation to dispense with God and to abandon all practical belief in life hereafter. Moreover it is possible for *disorderly tendencies,* of an individual or social nature, to develop within this same effort directed toward self-fulfillment. For instance, work itself is in need of salvation, and sexuality itself must be transcended.

Within these perspectives, the importance of the "spirituality of the cross" and the "spirituality of eschatology" becomes clear.

Christians will respond to this need of the modern world, a need that is equally pressing but less universally recognized, by the *testimony of their detachment.* Although the latter may adopt more accessible forms of moderation, it remains all the more striking when accepting the invitation to follow the evangelical counsels of voluntary poverty, of celibacy, virginity and of obedient service rendered to the kingship of God.

The pressing nature of the third form of testimony is frequently the least apparent in terms of psychology, but once its importance has been recognized, we are bound to acknowledge that the *testimony of prayer* remains the most vital from the ontological point of view. For how, indeed, can we assess human values according to their "relative" significance in an authentically Christian conception of life, if the relationship existing between these values and God is not made ex-

plicit in prayer? It is true that in this context likewise
certain modalities prove to be more "modern" than
others. The man who belongs to this technological age
is less inclined to experience a need for prayer in his
search for material benefits since he is aware that they
normally depend on physical laws and technical processes based on positive data. Nevertheless, he is capable of understanding the necessity of a prayer through
which *he asks that God may act within him and his
fellowmen,* so that human encounters may become more
effective and even more perfect in themselves. If he is
willing to take one step further, modern prayer becomes
above all a *prayer of communion* with God. It therefore appears providential that within the Church we are
participating at present in a revival of biblical medita-
tion and liturgical celebration.

Yet, this prayer, which from a certain point of view
truly represents the height of the encounter between
God and mankind in Jesus Christ, can never be considered as a definite *halting point. For the encounter
with God discovered in the sacred context seeks to
prolong its radiance into the encounter with God redis-
covered in the profane context and above all in our
neighbor.*

The term *"spirituality of redemption"* is interpreted
by us as being the most complete Christian attitude in
the sense indicated by the above scheme of ideas. In
considering the incarnation, the cross and the resurrection as a unique mystery possessing a dynamic character,
a Christian is founding both his thought and his behavior
upon the essential.

In this way, we are able to avoid defects inherent in
certain stresses made by more biased types of spirituality.

Above all, we can reorient those tendencies, which when exaggerated lead to the two forms of atheism mentioned above, and place them on the right course. Men allow themselves to drift toward the sin of absolute anthropocentricity either because they consider God as a rival to their autonomy or because they seek to make God serve them. Redemption in Jesus Christ affords us both the vision and the strength to cooperate with him in our conversion to theocentricity and participation: Christians desire to live *in the service of God* and *in union with God*. They are confident that they will find their true happiness through the acknowledgment of their fundamental dependence and through participation in the very life of God which is communicated to them by Christ.

By discovering in redemption both the truth and the strength of Christ *as an expression and a radiation of charity,* we achieve the point of contact between prayer and action. A Christian's life is spent in this love of God, a love of which he is the beneficiary, a love which he is capable of reciprocating. He loves God himself, as Jesus has revealed him and as he is encountered in the living Christ.

Following the example of Jesus, and living with him, a Christian is united to God in love by obeying his will. And this *will of God is equally incarnated in the effort which God expects of man* who seeks to promote human values both as an individual and as a member of society. This effort is of "relative" significance, as we have already pointed out on several occasions, but it represents wholehearted commitment to life in the world according to the relative autonomy of each level of existence which has its own effectiveness and its specific rhythm. It is *an effort "quickened"* by the Spirit of Christ. It renders us capable of transforming all our actions, and with increasing perfection, into practical applications of charity. Of all material mediations, mutual assistance is often the most clearly indicated; and unification, both universal and pluralist, appears as the most modern form of social conditioning. But neither provide a definite solution. For the supreme value which must be realized, the factor most clearly embodied in mutual aid and other mediations such as dialogue, is the *dynamism of interpersonal communion.* This power of communion which constitutes charity itself, transcends mere human reality in order to participate in *the love in which the Father, the Son and the Holy Spirit live united.*

C. The Structures of a Catechesis Starting from Human Realities

In the present context, we are considering a type of catechesis dealing with human realities which must be elucidated by the Christian message and transformed by the power of grace. This type is therefore directly connected with the question of "human conditioning" examined above.

We must recall nonetheless that the first type of catechesis, namely the one starting from the Word of God and concerning which the subdivisions have been indicated in Chap. II; equally takes human conditioning into account. Accordingly, we have laid special emphasis on the influence of Semitic conditioning, throughout the history of redemption.

Moreover, within the context of the second type of catechesis, and particularly at such times as we have to underline criteria of judgment, the ontological priority of the word of God is reaffirmed. We have distinguished two subdivisions in this second type: I. events (which are in a more or less unexpected way incorporated in situations)—and II. living problems (relating to values which must be realized in a fairly permanent way).

Events must be *considered in relation to the existential situation of a man who is summoned to progress more and more toward the kingdom and the salvation offered by Jesus Christ.* We must pay particular attention to the question of *conversion* since, through the latter, events are understood and accepted in a different sense than they appear to a man who refuses the gift of God's salvation.

The following structure has been adopted in Chap. III:

1. *Examining the contemporary situation.* The experience of autonomy and solidarity; the need for realism.

Distinguishing possible orientations, particularly with regard to religion.

2. *Passing a judgment.* The temptation of atheism is based either on human self-sufficiency or on failure to trust God. *Defining the criteria and the answer:* Jesus Christ delivers man from this double form of anthropocentricity; he summons him to effect a definite transcendence and grants him the necessary strength.

3. *Transforming our mentality and our actions.* Acceptance of the gospel of salvation by a threefold testimony of faith: prayer, poverty, charity. *Contemporary application according* to a different kind of psychological order but leading to an authentic spirituality of redemption.

D. Complementary Questions

Having reached the end of this recapitulatory chapter, we trust that its contents will have covered all essential points and in sufficient detail. Our confidence, however, does not allow us to forget that a large number of important questions relating to redemption have not received explicit answers. These must therefore be developed in greater or lesser detail according to the requirements, but they must always refer to the essential.

To conclude, let us single out the most important of these questions concerning modern conditioning and the principle to be adopted in their answer.

The conditioning factors of modern man, examined explicitly in the previous pages, referred directly to environments that are fairly well developed from the technological point of view, and to the choice that man can effect between drifting gradually but ever more surely toward atheistic humanism, and consciously welcoming salvation in Jesus Christ.

But among contemporary situations that have a different connotation we can select four examples:

1. *The Affluent Society and Salvation*

This example represents a further stage in our examination of environments fairly well developed from the technological point of view. The affluent man is less inclined to exercise his dynamic strength than to stagnate; he is less prepared to exhibit a sense of solidarity than to withdraw within his own group. Following this direction, he is bound to neglect his need for salvation.

He must be reawakened to the meaning of the human defects implied in his situation, helped in his task of controlling affluence in a human manner, and encouraged to respond to transcendence which is his true destiny in terms of happiness.

2. *Environments Technically not yet Developed*

At the other extreme, a great proportion of the world population has not yet undergone the experience previously designated as one of human autonomy opposed to religion, nor is it yet familiar with the experience of effective universal solidarity. Moreover it remains still unaware of that particular need for realism which abolishes the majority of superstitions inherent in the demiurgic mentality.

The path these nations must follow toward Christian salvation does of course raise the question of specific requirements, namely: (1) contact with Christian testimony to human aid, in all its aspects, this assistance being provided by the situation of Western countries which are more favored from the technological point of view; (2) the possibility of comparing cultural forms adopted up till now by Christianity with those prevailing in non-Western countries. This path, however, equally links up with the central problem of contact between the gospel of salvation and human promotion founded on a technically developed civilization which they will soon adopt as their own.

3. *Encounter between Different Religions, and the Latters' Present Task*

Once again, we must stress the fact that in our present society this question is directly related to technological development. On the one hand, a worldwide movement of technological unification is responsible for closer and more frequent physical contact between the followers of different religions. On the other, non-Christian faiths, as well as other Christian denominations, are obliged to "revise" their attitude when faced with the fact of man's technological power and the results he achieves.

In making this revision, a distinction must be made between the factors contained in these religions having an insufficient foundation, and those corresponding to the true religious nature of man in the context of a given culture. Hence the need for a new attitude of dialogue in announcing the gospel of salvation in order to discover which factors can be interpreted as a positive state of preparedness in welcoming Christian revelation.

In our attempt to define what salvation in Jesus Christ can signify to men who profess a different faith, we should accordingly seek to discover how these religions envisage salvation. For example, in *Recherches et Débats* 37 (1961) Fayard, we may consult the answers provided by the major religions concerning their attitude toward elements of "salvation": the struggle against social injustice, the promotion of cultural values, the development of a world community, inner life. See Brandon, *The Saviour God. Comparative Studies in the Concept of Salvation* (Manchester Univ. Press, 1963.)

In this way, the proclamation of Christian redemption will follow the essential dialectic movement and reveal the gospel as an extension of all good elements, as a discontinuity which requires man's conversion, and as a transcendence giving access to fulfillment.

4. *Anonymous Christianity*

The points we have just made on preparation for Christian conversion no doubt cover a wider sphere than certain similarities in thought and behavior. Paradoxically, an opposition to certain forms usually adopted by Christianity may stem from a deeply rooted need for truth and charity, which constitutes a more real and effective state of preparedness than the one provided by superficial points of agreement.

Thus, many individuals may find themselves "on the road" to Christianity, even without being aware of this fact. The authentic message of Christ will accordingly awaken this initial and unconscious faith to explicit and ever-increasing knowledge. In this case, we speak of "anonymous Christianity" but in the primary sense of a man who is journeying toward Christ.

Can we also speak of "anonymous Christianity" in a fuller sense and assert that many men of good-will are already truly Christian without their knowledge? Could Christ's salvation have already reached them unaware? Here we must make a distinction founded precisely on the difference we have indicated at great length above and which exists between absolute anthropocentricity and an awareness of the need for God's salvation. If the term "good-will" implies a self-sufficient humanism, this particular attitude is by no means Christian. At the very most, it might represent a stage in a journey which will reveal man's inability to suffice unto himself if he is to remain faithful to his true destiny. If, on the other hand, good-will denotes responsiveness to God, in the awareness that we need God for our salvation— an awareness which may be vague perhaps, but sufficient to allow for real humility and trust in God— then man can find room within him for the faith required by salvation, a faith which though implicit really transcends earthly supports, a faith which can already welcome Christ before his name is known.

The development of this attitude must principally follow the direction of charity, for charity reveals itself most clearly as a need and a capacity for transcending human imperfections. Provided that this dynamic force is not conceived distortedly as an inclination to pantheism, it will constitute the essential attitude to recognize and welcome a personal God who is love and has manifested this love by sending his Son, Jesus Christ, to save us and bring us into full communion with him.